POUR the OIL

ACCESS THE OIL, ACTIVATE THE POWER

Thea Harris

Thea Harris Publishing, Inc.
Port St Lucie, Florida

All scripture quotations, unless otherwise indicated, are taken from the Holy Bible, New International Version®, NIV®. Copyright ©1973, 1978, 1984, 2011 by Biblica, Inc.™ Used by permission of Zondervan. All rights reserved worldwide. www.zondervan.com The "NIV" and "New International Version" are trademarks registered in the United States Patent and Trademark Office by Biblica, Inc.™

Scripture quotations marked (AMP) are taken from the Amplified Bible, Copyright © 1954, 1958, 1962, 1964, 1965, 1987 by The Lockman Foundation. Used by permission.

Scripture taken from the New King James Version®. Copyright © 1982 by Thomas Nelson. Used by permission. All rights reserved.

Scripture quotations marked (NLT) are taken from the Holy Bible, New Living Translation, copyright © 1996, 2004, 2007 by Tyndale House Foundation. Used by permission of Tyndale House Publishers, Inc., Carol Stream, Illinois 60188. All rights reserved.

Scripture quotations marked ESV® Bible are taken from the Holy Bible, English Standard Version®) copyright © 2001 by Crossway, a publishing ministry of Good News Publishers. ESV® Text Edition: 2011. The ESV® text has been reproduced in cooperation with and by permission of Good News Publishers.

Scripture quotations marked ERV, Copyright © 2006 by World Bible Translation Center. Used by permission.

All definitions are found in Merriam Webster's Dictionary unless otherwise specified.

Front Cover Photo © 2014 by Shenneth Canegata for Heavenly Designs Graphics

Back Cover Photo © 2013 by Cearena Sweeney for DocuMemories Photography

Library of Congress Control Number: 2014919058

Copyright © 2014 by Anthea C. Harris
All rights reserved.
This book or parts thereof may not be reproduced in any form, stored in a retrieval system, or transmitted in any form by any means - electronic, mechanical, photocopy, recording or otherwise - without prior written permission of the publisher, except as provided by United States of American copyright law.
Published by Thea Harris Publishing * P.O. Box 7576
Port St. Lucie, FL 34985 * www.theaharris.com.

ISBN-13: 978-0990917007

ISBN-10: 0990917002

DEDICATION

This book is dedicated to my husband, Bruce
for his unwavering love and commitment
during my process.

CONTENTS

ACKNOWLEDGMENTS

Thank you to those God used to inspire this book, through their questions and comments about the anointing.

Special thanks to Apostle Trevor Banks & Pastor Martha Banks for spiritual guidance, and for allowing the oil to saturate their lives.

They are examples of stalwart Kingdom warriors who serve in an overflow of the anointing.

Thank you to Racquel Henry for her editorial services

FOREWORD

Pour the Oil is an insightful guide delineating a spiritual journey that begins with the conception of kingdom seed in the heart. The kingdom seed travels through tests and trials designed to cause germination, climaxing in the anointing that destroys every yoke and stature in the spirit that represents our Heavenly Father fully. We are predestined to be conformed to the image of God's son Jesus. As the Oil is poured upon us and reaches a saturation point, both we and the environment around us are impacted and changed from glory to glory.

Pour the Oil identifies stumbling blocks, snares and pitfalls hidden along the path toward destiny, while outlining steps to protection and purification that position us to be a carrier of His presence, His anointing. I enthusiastically recommend "Pour the Oil" as a must read. A book written through the pure inspiration of the Holy Spirit. It will powerfully impact the body of Christ.

The wisdom found in the pages of this book will arm you to fight the good fight of faith and manifest growth in grace and the knowledge of our Lord and Savior Jesus Christ. Sister Thea you have been a joy to shepherd. We are proud of you. We pray that the good work God is doing in you and producing for the body of Christ through you will continue until we arrive home at the place known as "Destiny."

Apostle Trevor Banks, Senior Pastor
Resurrection Life Family Worship Center, Inc

INTRODUCTION

Ministering without the anointing from the Anointed One (Jesus) is like stepping on the front line of battle with no armor. Do you want to identify issues that block its flow and develop principles to cultivate and enhance it in your life? Do you have a strong desire to minister under the fullness of its power? Has your gift been well received yet seems to make no spiritual impact? *Pour the Oil* is an insightful guide to help you determine root causes for the absence of the anointing and provide tools to get the oil flowing again.

If you were pouring clean water into a crystal glass and saw flecks of dirt swirling around in it as you poured; what would you do? Would you drink from a contaminated utensil or would you empty that glass and wash it thoroughly before pouring again? I imagine even after washing you would inspect the glass to make sure all of the dirt had been removed before beginning to pour again. You would watch carefully until you were absolutely sure no dirt remained. Most people never willingly drink water unless they know without a doubt it is clean. You are like that glass, and the Holy Spirit pours the water of the Word to expose hidden contaminants and to cleanse. God carefully examines your heart to ensure you are truly ready to carry the anointing.

In the days of Noah, it was necessary to cover the whole earth with water to destroy the people. They had become evil and wicked in the sight of God and it troubled His heart. Noah was spared because he was found worthy. He had been anointed for purpose.

The Bible says that "Noah was a righteous man, blameless among the people of his time, and he walked faithfully with God" (Genesis 6:9). His family was spared because of his heart, his anointing and his purity. God established a covenant with Noah, covering his entire family (Genesis 6:18).

To be effective as a prophet, king or a priest, decide to be a worthy vessel. Sometimes you will be purified by fire. Peter admonishes, "For a little while you may have had to suffer grief in all kinds of trials. These have come so that your faith--of greater worth than gold, which perishes even though refined by fire--may be proved genuine and may result in praise, glory and honor when Jesus Christ is revealed" (1 Peter 1:6-7). The fire can either be sent by God or He allows it for your benefit.

A strong anointing poured into a dirty vessel is harmful both to the carrier and to all of the lives they serve. When God desires to use you, consecration is a requirement. You must become a vessel, worthy to wear the Mantle; qualified to carry the anointing. Keep yourself pure. Walk in purpose and positively impact those assigned to you. Make a decision to cleanse your soul to carry a pure anointing, and do it. That guarantees a life of victory. Your destiny will be fulfilled.

Shadrach, Meshach and Abednego would only worship the one true God, even when threatened with death. God allowed Nebuchadnezzar to throw them into the midst of a fire, but He protected their garments and their bodies from the wrath of the flames (Daniel 3).

Pure spirits are adorned and protected in the fire, by the presence of the Holy Spirit. While the Hebrew boys walked around in the flames, they continued to pray and worship while the ones who tried to harm them perished (Daniel 3:22-25). God did not forsake them, and He will not forsake you.

The devil has no authority over a devoted worshiper. He cannot block the move of God in your life. Experiences (negative or positive) are part of your spiritual definition. Who you become determines what you will allow or disallow.

Shadrach, Meshach and Abednego would not worship false gods. Their stand caused Nebuchadnezzar to acknowledge God and proclaim to the entire Kingdom, "Praise be to the God of Shadrach, Meshach and Abednego, who has sent his angel and rescued his servants! They trusted in him, defied the king's command and were willing to give up their lives rather than serve or worship any god except their own God. Therefore I decree that the people of any nation or language who say anything against the God of Shadrach, Meshach and Abednego be cut into pieces and their houses be turned into piles of rubble, for no other god can save in this way" (Daniel 3:28-29).

Pour the Oil identifies contaminants that make you ineffective. It outlines steps for purification that will position you to be the worshiper God seeks. It also teaches how to arm yourself to fight the ultimate spiritual battle, attain your value as a Kingdom warrior and garner the blessing of your Heavenly Father. Like Jesus Christ, you too can hear God say, "This is my Son, whom I love; with him I am well pleased" (Matthew 3:17). Prepare to be anointed. Answer God's call. Allow Him to equip you for Kingdom purpose. Qualify for the Blessing of the Dove (Holy Spirit). Open your heart to transformation power as God pours the oil over you.

Chapter One

PREPARING FOR THE OIL

God told Jeremiah, "Before I formed you in the womb I knew you, before you were born I set you apart; I appointed you as a prophet to the nations" (Jeremiah 1:5). When you are set apart at a really young age, there are trials and tribulations that you are not yet equipped to handle. The enemy seeks to contaminate your soul before you are fully mature. He wants to destroy you so that your life's purpose is never realized. I know this to be true from personal experience.

For a long time, I could not understand the trials I endured in my young life or identify their purpose. Why was my heart fractured or broken, and haphazardly put back together only to be broken again? Why was the fight so fierce? Eventually I found answers, through revelation, and over time. Now, when I minister as a worshipper, invariably someone asks, "How can I get the anointing?" A short answer is impossible. There are major truths that must be understood. The anointing does not come overnight and it will cost you.

God found me at age thirteen. By sixteen, although I was not alone, I was lonely and struggling to find my identity. I had friends who did not know my struggle. My heart would not connect with many of my peers. I felt lost and insecure, but even then I knew it was important to wash myself in the Word.

Loneliness and uncertainty made me feel desperate for human connection, but the people I eventually connected with were not sent by God. They were sent by the enemy. He took a

5

heart that was already vulnerable and assigned his agents to further distort self perception. He tried to gain a permanent stronghold in my life. Through all of my mistakes and mess-ups, I was burying my head in the Bible for hours at a time, seeking solace, seeking direction—seeking God.

I enlisted in the U. S. Army after high school. I made friends with other soldiers, but every weekend, instead of using my off-base pass to go into the city to party, I went to an outreach ministry called Victory Ranch. Each Friday Ma & Pa Bear (that's what they called themselves) picked me up at the base. At the Ranch, we worshiped, studied the Word and fellowshipped with one another. I was still seeking solace, seeking direction, seeking God.

By age twenty-two I ended military service, married and enrolled in college. At twenty-four, I gave birth to a precious baby girl. Sadly the marriage did not work, and I became a single mom. Throughout this entire journey I could feel deep in my soul that there was something missing in my life. I carried deep hurts, but God kept drawing me to Him. I knew to seek Him, but somehow I became polluted with contaminants. I was reading the Word, but not fully obeying it. My natural desire for connection and fellowship kept superseding the spiritual need to accurately connect with God.

Contaminants sickened my soul until it became a fierce struggle to get back to that place where the sweetness of the Holy Spirit washed over me daily. It took almost ten years of a raging and continuous battle, but the call on my life had begun before the storm. It was stronger than the conflict that threatened to consume me.

I slowly journeyed back to God. In the place called full surrender, I accepted the fact that God truly loved me. He had a purpose for my life. When I said yes to my Heavenly Father, I began the painful process of detoxifying my spirit of all the hurts that had created fear, an unforgiving attitude, pride and offense. I also had to expunge the stain and stench that guilt over disobedience had formed as a dark, heavy, shroud over my spirit. King David asked, "How long, O LORD? Will you hide yourself forever?" (Psalm 89:46). *I* felt like King David, but God was not hiding from me. He was drawing me in, I just could not see. He was saying "I have loved you with an everlasting love; I have drawn you with unfailing kindness," (Jeremiah 31:3) but I could not hear. My soul was contaminated.

My spirit had shriveled, much like the fig tree Christ cursed because it was unfruitful, but He had not cursed me. He kept trying to cradle me, but I did not know how to receive His love. I did not know I was lovable, but He did. He kept calling me, drawing me in, and loving me anyway. He removed the scales from my eyes, and I saw myself in the mirror of His Word.

Only after surrendering and submitting to Christ's will did my anointing manifest. I had to allow God to remove the toxins and purify me for service. After identifying the contaminants one by one, I asked Him to wash me, cleanse me, and make me fit for purpose. I wanted to be prepared for destiny.

IDENTIFY THE CONTAMINANTS

Contaminants serve a single purpose, to weaken and render you powerless. They present themselves as a result of experiences that distort and destroy your imagination and reality. It is similar to a healthy human cell becoming infected by cancer. If cancer cells do not die, they become malignant and destroy healthy cells. This begins a state of decline in the body unless unhealthy cells are attacked and destroyed.[1]

Recognizing and destroying contaminants is the only way to ensure they do not become malignant. They aggressively and maliciously attack and eventually kill your spirit, and then your soul. It is important to identify them and begin to violently and thoroughly remove them so there are no hindrances or limitations in your spiritual life.

God gave the Prophet Isaiah a vision for the people of Israel. This vision exposed how they had allowed themselves to become contaminated and turned their backs on God. Their spiritual condition was frightening. God told Isaiah, "The whole head is sick, and the whole heart faint. From the sole of the foot even unto the head there is no soundness in it; but wounds, and bruises, and putrefying sores: they have not been closed, neither bound up, neither mollified with ointment"

(Isaiah 1:5-6).

When people are in this state, Satan has the most power. He uses them to propagate the works of the flesh. They are hindered from entering the presence of God. Contaminants like pride, unforgiveness, fear, flesh, offense, disobedience, and a lack of faith clog spiritual pores and suffocate until purpose and destiny are unattainable. Eliminate them and avoid undesirable end results.

Pride and Unforgiveness
Pride blinds you to internal struggles and shortcomings because you refuse to examine yourself. You may think you are alright, and everyone else needs fixing. The Bible says, "pride goeth before destruction, and an haughty spirit before a fall" (Proverbs 16:18, KJV). An individual who is prideful develops a stiff neck so they can feel right about everything or feel superior to others. In Acts chapter seven, Apostle Stephen called the Sanhedrin "stiff necked people whose hearts and ears are uncircumcised; who always resist the Holy Spirit" (Verse 51). After Stephen made that statement to the Sanhedrin, he was stoned to death.

Pride not only blocks you from hearing others, you also cannot hear God. It is difficult to forgive others of their limitations and inadequacies. You would rather walk down a wrong path before taking advice from someone. A prideful person accepts no responsibility when they realize their mistake. Rather, they blame someone else. Pride is a terrible contaminant. It binds others up with wrong accusations. It is fueled by anger and bitterness.

Pride yields to no one, not even God (Psalms 10:4). It is a dangerous poison and makes you easy prey for the devil. It is not difficult to receive the thoughts he whispers in your heart when you are full of pride and unforgiveness. Forgive quickly and completely. Humble yourself before the Lord (James 4:10) and become fit for Kingdom service.

Too Proud To Forgive
You must guard against pride. It can manifest itself in a number of ways. You can be too proud to ask for forgiveness.

When the profound process to wholeness begins, you are fragile. You rely on God for everything and give Him credit for all He is doing. Do not become a walking contradiction, speaking about God's love with others, yet not loving enough to release those who hurt you. This leads to stored anger and bitterness.

These emotions block the move of God and keep you connected to your past. They prevent you from being able to let go of feelings associated with bad experiences. You hold others prisoner with your will and emotions. James 1:20 warns us, "human anger does not produce the righteousness that God desires." Choosing not to forgive is a perilous choice (Mark 11:25). It affects your heart and prayer life.

When God called me back into ministry, I started fostering a friendship with someone (*let's call her Beatrice*) who eventually became offended by me in some way. I still have no idea what I had done, but I was hurt by how she reacted. Without warning or reason, she stopped speaking to me. Beatrice closed herself off completely, and acted as if I were her enemy.

I felt angry that I created an opportunity for her to get close. This situation was so troubling, during worship one Sunday morning, I said to God, "I am going to ask Beatrice what I have done" and He said, "You will not! What you need to do is find her after service and say you're sorry." "Whoa God, but I haven't done anything wrong. What will I be apologizing for?" He simply repeated, "What you need to do is find her after service and say that *you* are sorry." God made it clear that I did not need to know the reason for her actions; I simply needed to forgive. I was obedient and as I said "I am sorry" it felt like a weight lifted from my heart. When I walked out of the room, I was at peace. Beatrice's reasons no longer mattered. I could minister with a pure heart.

It is possible Beatrice was reacting out of her own hurts, and my questions could have caused further harm. Sometimes you have to forgive even when others may not forgive you. She never said much to me afterwards, but I could smile and say hello each time I saw her. Out of the experience, God gave me the capacity to love others the way He does. In Matthew 22:37-38 Jesus said, "Love the Lord your God with all your heart and with all your soul and with all your mind. This is the first and greatest commandment. And the second is like it: 'Love your neighbor as yourself.'" The ability to do this draws an anointing which cannot be manufactured.

Taking Credit for God's Work

Pride can also manifest when you get off track and begin taking credit for the things God is doing through you. The arrogant think of themselves as invincible. They allow the spirit of pride to consume them.

It made Lucifer lose his stature. He said in his heart "I will ascend to the heavens; I will raise my throne above the stars of God; I will sit enthroned on the mount of assembly, on the utmost heights of Mount Zaphon. I will ascend above the tops of the clouds; I will make myself like the Most High" (Isaiah 14:12-14). God's response was rapid expulsion (Luke 10:18).

You position yourself for the same response if you take credit for the work God does through you. Lucifer gloried in himself and the influence of his anointing. He was no longer satisfied with serving; He wanted power. Instead he became the devil, your enemy. Guard your heart against pride.

Pride Kills the Anointing

Without the anointing; manifested works have a demonic component. They are fleeting and it is only a matter of time before degradation is exposed. Pharaoh's pride and stubbornness caused him to resist Moses' request to free his people. Moses was anointed for that task. Pharaoh's sorcerers had a gift to perform similar acts, but there was no anointing from God. They relied on witchcraft to mimic and reproduce something that looked anointed. They tried to intimidate Moses so Pharaoh could feel justified when he continued to hold the people of Israel in captivity (Exodus 7:11).

Moses had not moved in his own strength or tried to advance his agenda. God sent him to Egypt (Exodus 9:1). Pharaoh, on the other hand, simply sought power. It did not matter that his power source was evil. His main objective was maintaining control. Be careful not to allow the desire to be in control to rule your spirit. That is not God's way; it is Satan's.

No good thing can come of it.

Another example of a manifested demonic component was the instance where the prophets of Baal tried proving that Baal was the one true God, yet all calls to him were futile. All pleadings went unanswered. In desperation they resorted to perverted antics that still yielded no result (1 Kings 18:26-29).

Baal's prophets were desperate. The silence amplified the powerlessness of their false god. Desperation led to twisted measures which did not help. If you do not develop a strong relationship with God, you can find yourself in the same situation. You will seek answers in the wrong places and make bad decisions when there is no answer. The following emptiness leads to a place of fear. Don't allow fear to drive you.

Fear and the Flesh
The spirit of fear infects. It is like an insidious predator that permeates the soul and infuses itself into the spirit of the unsuspecting. It brings contamination, and fleshly attitudes and behaviors manifest. It is difficult for someone infected by fear to rely on the Word of God because fear consumes them. It invades thoughts, feelings, words and actions.

Fear reacts from a raw, emotional place and does not consider, but pounces. This spirit is dangerous to the spiritual health and growth of an individual, and God admonishes over and over again to fear not (2 Timothy 1:7). A person living in fear does not have peace of mind. If you let the spirit of fear overtake; complete deliverance is needed to become totally free.

Fear begins alone, but picks up friends along the way. It walks hand in hand with other emotions that relentlessly torture the soul. First, it causes wrong actions or responses. Rehearsed wrongs bring guilt, and guilt brings condemnation. Condemnation causes torment, and fear grows in torment until it grips the soul. It controls the mind and contaminates the heart. It overtakes common sense and superimposes irrational, sometimes fantasy based projections about what could happen. It cripples and produces procrastination and false predictions.

Once fear is allowed to take hold, it brings along depression and oppression. You are unable to move, act, or think clearly. You exist in a cloud of *what ifs* and *I can't(s)*.

The spirit of fear is primal. It moves instinctively. The person who lives in fear has a narrow perspective. It is difficult to convince them that anything other than what they feel is possible. The Prophet Elijah performed many miracles under the power of God, but a few words spoken by a tyrant queen (Jezebel) made him run for his life. He wanted to die because her words gripped his heart with fear (I Kings 19:1-4). Not even the manifested works of God in and through him caused reason to rule. Fear infiltrated and contaminated Elijah.

An individual afflicted by fearful thoughts sees the worst in every situation; therefore they think the worst. Fear dominates. Someone who is fearful sees disaster, even in the good. To them, there is an enemy lurking in every corner. Everything looks threatening; everything feels wrong. They believe that everything will go wrong. Often they are not aware that their entire thought process is guided by fear and it becomes a way of life.

When fear overshadows a soul, it pushes away everything that is positive. It insinuates until doubt comes. Fearful words spew out of the mouth unbridled. If it cannot convince, it manipulates with words that hurt, demean, discourage, or cause a perspective of defeat to manifest. If allowed, it even punctures shields of faith. The spirit is not governing.

Fear represses love. Love and fear cannot co-exist. One destroys while the other nurtures. The widow at Zarephath loved her son; but fear caused her to speak a prophetic word of death over him (I Kings 17: 12). Her faith could not operate, because of fear. She saw, felt, thought and spoke all of the wrong words over their lives because of fear. Her vocabulary conveyed hopelessness and resignation to a fate she did not want. She felt powerless to speak against her situation because of fear. It was the encounter with Elijah that saved her life and restored the life of her son.

Fear has room to grow because it distorts focus and shifts purpose. The first thing Elijah said to the widow was, "Don't be afraid." He attacked her fear with words. He then gave her a task that helped to break the spirit of fear (I Kings 17: 13). The widow's focus was no longer on her situation, now she was being asked to do something for someone else. Her purpose shifted from merely performing a final task before death to providing sustenance and life to the prophet Elijah.

Fear kills the anointing. When Christ bid Peter to come, he walked on water. The anointing gave him both the faith and the power to move. When Peter allowed fear to enter in and become his focus, it killed the anointing. Not even the Presence of Christ could protect it; Peter could only be rescued.

Like Peter, sometimes you invite God to act, but have no faith. He extends mercy when fear reduces your courage (Matthew 14:22-33).

Fear hides in anger. Fear masks itself with anger. Anger produces a feeling of invincibility. It deceives you into believing that you are right, no matter your course of action. When fear lodged into the subconscious mind of Joseph's brothers, they felt threatened by the *possibility* that he could actually rule them. This fear was fed by their father's preference for Joseph and his outward show of favoritism. Joseph certainly did not help when he reported them to his father. The only way they could be sure what they feared would never became reality was to get rid of him. Fear introduced murderous thoughts. Anger provoked wicked actions (Genesis 37:3-11).

Fear aborts your process. Premature birthing forms abnormalities in spiritual vision. Instead of moving toward God's divine plan for your life, you detour based on a defective vision. You become infected by fear and a malformed purpose hurts you. The outworking of this deformity is stagnation as a result of continuous procrastination. You cannot move. You keep putting things off. You fear the process, the people, the outcomes, and the responsibilities created by success. You are afraid of fear itself. Left untreated, fear is allowed to fester and purpose is never fulfilled.

Fear blocks success. It keeps it at bay until you become a shell of your former self, broken and bitter because your dreams are unrealized. Fear causes you to open doors that should be shut and close doors that should be open. You let people in that should be kept out and keep out those you should let in. Do not become a prisoner of fear. Forgive yourself and learn how to progress beyond its barriers. You will not move forward if you live in fear.

An individual who lives in fear moves purely in the flesh, because the spirit cannot rule when fear dominates. Elijah was a spiritual giant, yet he ran because Jezebel threatened him. He not only ran, but he asked God to take his life. There was no spirit operating there; he lost power because of fear.

Paul said, "I die every day" (1 Corinthians 15:31). Dying to the flesh means completely relying on God. That reliance causes you to focus on His Word. He is your blessed assurance. Christ conquered death and the grave. You have nothing to fear.

Fear creates emotional deformity and spiritual fractures that bend or break your will. Deformed emotions create unhealthy self concepts and misguided perceptions of experiences and of people. Spiritual fractures give Satan room to seep in and begin a process of erosion. Eventually fear controls the mind. Those who are controlled become walking contradictions, volleying between flesh and spirit. The Apostle Paul said,

> For I do not understand my own actions [I am baffled, bewildered]. I do not practice or accomplish what I wish, but I do the very thing that I loathe [which my moral instinct condemns]. Now if I do [habitually] what is contrary to my desire, [that means that] I acknowledge and agree that the Law is good (morally excellent) and that I take sides with it (Romans 7:15-16, AMP).

What a torturous existence. This is the way you live when governed by fear, constantly vacillating and hating yourself for it. Condemnation takes up residence in your heart, and it does not relinquish territory easily. Like fear it seeks to remain. A life of fear and condemnation is no life at all. You must build your spirit up and allow it to rule.

Fear awakens misgivings. Those misgivings superimpose themselves over your spirit and influence your decisions—fear of being alone, fear of not having enough, fear of not having the approval of others, fear of failure, and fear of success. These fears access your base emotions and create a sanctuary for vacant thoughts and unmet needs. Your thinking becomes a weapon that produces self inflicted wounds. Your emotions are wounded and your will is controlled by the devil. You are led by fear.

Fear kills faith. Elijah ran because fear crept in and killed his belief in God's power to save him. He no longer felt capable of manifesting The Power because Jezebel scared him. He could have spoken as he had in times past and watched the power of God manifest.

You have to speak in faith until you believe. The Shunamite woman kept her dream alive, because she said repeatedly, "it is well" even though her son was dead, "it is well," and her heart was broken, "it is well," and she was in despair, "it is well" (2 Kings 4:26-27, KJV). Fear may have tried to grip her heart, but she focused on keeping faith alive by killing it with words. It had no place to go, and her dream became alive again.

Do not entertain a spirit of fear. Focusing on it creates a dreadful reality. The Bible says, "For God has not given us a spirit of fear, but of power" (2 Timothy 1:7, KJV). Mediate on this scripture.

Job said, "What I feared has come upon me; what I dreaded has happened to me" (Job 3:25). He received fear and entertained it, and saw it come to life. He may have worried about losing what he had, or spoken of it. It is possible he rehearsed it in his mind over and over again until it became a part of his reality.

The Conception of Fear

Fear does not just happen. It is first conceived in the mind because of experiences and words that deeply affect the heart. The mind is literally your control center and the brain directs each area of your body. Your mind creates indecision or drives unhealthy, irrational and unwise decisions. It prevents you from acting when you should and causes you to act when you should not.

Have you considered what happens to a mind affected by

fear? Conceived fear is fed *or starved* by your thoughts. Depending on the influencing experience, killing fear once it has captured the imagination can be a great challenge. Thank God for the spirit who has the authority to control the soul. It is fed by the Spirit of God through equipping tools, which I will write about later in this chapter.

When fear is perpetually used to discipline children, it becomes normal for that person to make decisions based on fear in almost every situation they face. It is a part of who they are and determines how they live. Fear causes them to stay in old patterns, choking the life out of them. It is like a python that renders his prey immobile, swallowing and suffocating, liquefying bones so they cannot stand. It squeezes until the soul dies. The spirit diminishes, and eventually, the person dies.

Unidentified fear is like an undetected terminal illness, insidiously eating away at the soul until life ceases. It is important to identify fear in your life, because it affects you in ways that increase exposure and susceptibility to the enemy's promptings. You *must* remain aware so you can proactively work towards eliminating it from your life.

When you decide to get rid of fear, immediately a spiritual battleground is activated. It fosters land mines (*they explode suddenly and without warning*) or long range missiles (*projectiles that hit suddenly and without warning*) – both do major internal and external damage. The enemy pulls out all the stops to keep you in a position of weakness. He wants to be in complete control.

Wounds That Conceive Fear
Often those who are walking in fear carry deep wounds. They are bound by emotional lesions that stop spiritual growth by creating habits that keep them trapped in the past. Some wounds are caused by sexual abuse, repressed anger, low self esteem, a desire for validation, rejection, or the lack of a parent or other positive role model in the formative years. The stench of stagnation forms a shroud that ensnares the soul. This deformity drives every decision.

Sexual abuse – Tamar was raped by her brother Amnon. He

deceived and violated her (2 Samuel 13:6-18). Her spirit was broken and she never recovered from the shame and pain. She could not properly process what happened because Absalom insisted she be quiet about it. It is likely that he could not bear to hear it himself, and considered his own pain instead of Tamar's.

The Bible says that Tamar "lived in her brother Absalom's house, a desolate woman" (2 Samuel 13:20). Imagine being violated in such a violent way, then forced to internalize your pain. It consumed Tamar. She accepted her fate as a 'ruined' woman, and was fearful of the whispers, the disgrace, of her experience.

She was fearful of Amnon. Tamar was afraid to defy Absalom by speaking of her pain. She could not look into her father's eyes as he bore the shame of Amnon's sin. David could not ease her pain. He felt shame as he reflected on his inability to comfort his daughter, as he pondered his cowardice. He could not counsel Absalom about his feelings toward Amnon. Tamar became trapped and the experience defined her. Because of it, she had no future. She did not seek to forgive; or to heal.

Repressed anger. After Tamar's rape, King David repressed his anger. The Bible says that "he was furious" (2 Samuel 13:21) when he heard about it; yet he did nothing. David knew that if pushed, he could violently retaliate against Amnon. He was afraid that if he disciplined him their relationship would be ruined. He was afraid to see his daughter's brokenness or experience her anguish. He felt ill equipped to handle Absalom's rage. He was a conflicted man, and the already putrid situation was given time to fester.

Anger had the opposite effect on Absalom. It did not create fear. It caused him to make careless choices with explosive results. After nursing his rage for more than two years, Absalom ordered Amnon's murder (2 Samuel 13:28-29). An already dysfunctional situation became critical.

Repressed anger leads to acts of rebellion. Despite David's conquests on the battlefield, he was a coward in Absalom's eyes. Absalom believed David unworthy of the crown and therefore sought to take it from him (2 Samuel 15:1-10). Anger consumed Absalom until his spirit was grossly contaminated. He was a dishonorable son, a disloyal subject, a neglectful brother and a murderer. Anger also took him away from Tamar when he should have been helping her heal. He could no longer see what was important. All he saw were opportunities for revenge.

Repressed anger creates massive collateral damage. It is like a suicide bomber, a weapon of mass destruction, and everyone is at risk. Jacob's daughter Dinah was raped by Shechem the Hivite (Genesis 34). Unlike Tamar's situation, Shechem wanted to marry Dinah. She would regain honor through this union. Repressed anger blinded Jacob's sons to Shechem's good intentions. Rather than accept the offer, they secretly plotted revenge, using deception to manipulate all the young men of Hivite.

Shechem was told that if all the men were circumcised, he could marry Dinah. Circumcision was a sign of covenant in Israel (Genesis 17). That sacred act was used to physically weaken and kill the Hivite men, taking the women and children as slaves. Dinah's brothers became mass murderers who killed any opportunity for her honor to be restored (Genesis 34:30-31). Anger blinded them to the fact that their actions also put the entire nation at risk.

Dinah would be treated as a pariah all the days of her life. Although it is not clear what happened to her after she was taken back to her father's house, her future was likely the same as Tamar's—full of isolation, identity struggle, self hatred, self pity, low self esteem and hopelessness.

Low self esteem. Self esteem is defined as a, "sense of personal worth and ability that is fundamental to an individual's identity. The definition contains a reference to Karen Horney's assertion that low self-esteem leads to the development of a personality that excessively craves approval and affection," the key word being excessive. Excessive cravings provoke emotions that lead to negative assertions and responses. Satan will use them to bind you.

Low self esteem awakens the primal nature of fear. It

causes you to react inappropriately to people and situations. Saul wanted to kill David because he felt inadequate as a ruler. His jealousy was due to low self esteem. It made him view David as an adversary rather than a friend, but not because of anything David had done. Saul left the throne to pursue David, and he pulled others out of position to join him.

Saul was depressed and unstable. He called David to play his harp to soothe unease one moment, then tried killing him the next. Not even Saul's son, Jonathan, could dissuade him from trying to take David's life. If anything, it further fueled Saul's fear and anger. He believed David had also stolen his son's affection and approval (1 Samuel 18:1).

The devil uses low self esteem to play mind games. If he controls your mind, he controls you. God cannot commission you for Kingdom purpose until that stronghold is broken. There are many Christians in the church still struggling with low self esteem. They try to manipulate others with their will. It is a desperate quest for validation.

I gave others permission to shape me because I did not know who I was. I became a product of my insecurities, marrying someone I desired to share my life with and being wounded. Things in the marriage that caused my spirit to be broken existed from the beginning of the relationship. I just could not see them.

Low self esteem created great unrest in my spirit. I hardly ever stayed at a job for more than a year, not because I was incapable or because the jobs were undesirable, but because the enemy played mind games with me until I gave up and moved on.

Although I struggled with low self esteem, in my early twenties I became aware that God wired a fail-safe in my spirit from the time I was born. That fail-safe *suddenly* kicked in one day as I was looking at my face in the bathroom mirror. God began talking to me. He said, "what you see when you look at you is not what I created, but what others have said you are. You are seeing through the eyes of someone else. Do you see what I see? I see someone beautiful. You are beautiful. Say that until you believe it. *When* you believe, then you will begin to see it too."

That's Daddy God for you. He got straight to the point, "girl you've got blinders on." He told me to speak and *when* I believed (not *if*), then I would see. That was all part of the fail-safe. He knew it would activate the call to destiny and purpose. Wow. God is awesome.

Job said, "You shall also decide and decree a thing and it shall be established for you. And the light [of God's favor] shall shine upon your ways" (Job 22:28, AMP). I had not yet read that scripture, but God spoke it to my heart. Every time I walked by the mirror I looked at myself and said, "You are beautiful."

Don't get me wrong. I did not see what God was trying to show me right away, but I kept saying it. One day I started adding words. "Girl, you are beautiful; there is nothing wrong with you." My mind was being transformed and my spiritual eyes were opened. They saw what God saw when He looked at me. I could say, "I am lovable, and I am loved." This happened before I rededicated my life to God, so be encouraged. He will meet you where you are, heal your wounds, and make you brand new. Yield to His dealings in your life and let Him make you over.

You are special and God has a purpose for your life. He called me before I was in my mother's womb. The devil sought to distort my self-perception at a young age. He tried to cripple me mentally, emotionally and spiritually. The joke is on him though, because as I decided to believe, God allowed tough experiences. They were all part of my preparation for ministry. Look at Joseph, (Genesis 37, 39 – 50), he endured so much, and it was all to position him for his ultimate purpose.

All of your experiences have value. Ask God to show you how He wants to use them. Understanding will activate His call on your life. A stained glass window is made of broken or cut pieces, yet when they are put together; it is a thing of beauty. That is how God sees you. Every fracture, every break, every cut, fits perfectly somewhere in your transformation. Breaks create "forever change," but the finished work is marvelous.

Desire for Validation. Many wait a lifetime for validation that never comes. They are always looking, always needing, faltering, failing; accepting false offerings to alleviate hurts from past experiences. If you find yourself in such a place, watch your heart's attitude as you wait. Unmet needs deplete emotional resources. Eventually they become infected by anger, bitterness, and a spirit which seeks to dominate, manipulate and belittle others.

They push issues into the recesses of their heart; then pass on their need for validation to others. Now the individuals they attack and demean are constantly in need of validation too. It becomes a cycle until someone recognizes that although validation from their brethren has value, ultimately God's approval is most significant.

Lack of validation makes you vulnerable to wrong thoughts and actions. Cain expected validation from God for an offering he knew was displeasing. When he did not get it, he murdered his brother Abel in a jealous rage (Genesis 4:3-8). It is easy for people to misunderstand you and speak their misinterpretation as truth. Guard your heart from feeling overlooked. Instead, focus entirely on your call and purpose. Brave the looks, whispers and the criticisms by continuing to be real. See yourself as God does. Understand that more than anything or anyone, you need Him.

Rely on God; reduce the desire to actively and overtly solicit man's validation. If the yearning is not put in check, it begins to feed feelings of low self esteem. This increases the need for validation. The cycle is vicious and debilitating. It does not consider whether validation is deserved; it just craves it. Joseph's brothers felt that he was unworthy of their father's adoration. It drove them to the unthinkable (Genesis 37:4, 20, 28).

You must be accurately positioned to receive validation. Some want it although they are not qualified. David's son, Adonijah, had not been validated by his father; yet he attempted to highjack the throne, announcing himself as king (1 Kings 1:5). He was neither eligible nor anointed to rule God's people. On the other hand, Elisha, who graciously served Elijah, allowed himself to be developed through service (I Kings 19:19-21).

Validation is not only received as a result of works. It may also be given as acknowledgment of the anointing on someone's life. Elisha received a double portion of the anointing when Elijah's mantle fell, because he was committed to fulfilling purpose (2 Kings 2:11). Miracles he performed following Elijah's departure confirmed him as God's choice. Many witnessed the same magnified power in Elisha [that was seen in Elijah].

Validation from the right source is vital. Validation from the wrong source will weaken your anointing. Broken people seeking validation are like vacant buildings, empty, desolate, and open to all who seek to enter, even if they are bent on destruction. If you are yearning to be affirmed, it is critical to be careful about what you see, what you hear and from whom. When Adonijah tried to take the throne, one of the people he looked to for validation was Joab. He aligned himself with the same Joab who continually dishonored King David - Joab the miscreant, the murderer; Joab the rebellious.

It is dangerous to allow validation from the wrong source to define your self-concept. Adonijah connected with someone he was sure would validate wrongdoing rather than provide correction. He was surprised by the outcome. Instead of ruling a Kingdom he cowered in fear when his brother Solomon was crowned (1 Kings 1:49-51). Adonijah lost his life as a result of this error.

Validation from the right source propels you toward destiny. God validated Jesus after his baptism by John the Baptist (Matthew 3:16-17). Immediately, He was led to the wilderness to be tempted. He successfully resisted temptation and began preaching, teaching and performing miracles. Jesus aligned Himself with those who would help to accomplish His purpose (Matthew 4).

Premature movements stop the move toward destiny. If you have not gone through your process, and receive validation from the wrong source, it will destroy you like it destroyed Adonijah. The progression is: process, qualification, validation, purpose, and destiny. No one bypasses it.

The Bible says, "In all the work you are given, do the best you can. Work as though you are working for the Lord, not any earthly master" (Colossians 3:23, ERV). You want to perform assigned tasks to the satisfaction of earthly leaders, however if you only do it for man's validation, God cannot use you. Be careful not to see a lack of validation as outright rejection. It will derail you.

Rejection. Rejection causes a recipient to engage in behavior, which in their mind is designed to draw others to them, when in fact they are pushing them away. This creates another cycle, one of desperate and unreciprocated attempts to connect. The fear of not being accepted drives those unwanted efforts, when it is obviously neither desired nor appreciated. It is hard for someone stuck in this cycle to see it for what it is. There is almost a frenzied drive to make a connection happen. This causes the object of desired attachment to begin avoiding the individual. They harbor unkind thoughts which become unkind actions.

When I was in basic training at Fort Jackson, South Carolina, one of my fellow trainees was often the topic of negative conversation. People laughed at her, talked about her disparagingly (loud enough for her to hear) or ignored her. After some time, we could hear her talking to herself regularly. This only provided more ammunition for those who were attacking.

One Sunday morning she came to Chapel and as the guest soloist began singing, "Jesus Loves Me This I Know," I noticed that her face was bathed in tears, shoulders shaking with silent sobs that I could somehow feel. I understood that she was responding to the message of love. I would later learn it was something she longed for, something she needed desperately.

In your brokenness God causes you to develop empathy for the brokenness of others. When we returned to the Barracks, I smiled and said hello, and she began talking. She recounted a story of loss and immense pain. Her mother died when she was a young girl. Her father remarried and she felt unloved both by her stepmom and her dad. She was verbally and emotionally abused and had been repeatedly *rejected*. She repressed those emotions and when she entered basic training, as the physical and psychological rigors of our daily routine progressed, she became more and more unstable.

Her obvious instability generated even more rejection; this time from her peers. She succumbed to the pressure of that rejection. The Army discharged her, and I never saw her again. I like to think that the song about Jesus' love continued to work in her heart and she somehow found her way to Him.

Someone who is self assured celebrates the accomplishments of others. Saul could not celebrate David, because he thought the people's celebration of David clearly meant they rejected him (1 Samuel 18, 19). Rejection produced an anger that blinded Saul to anything other than the need to annihilate the one he blamed. It awakened fear; fear awakened anger. Anger provoked feelings of vengefulness. The need for revenge became Saul's new purpose. His focus shifted, which left a deficit in parenting responsibilities. His family was neglected. He withdrew love, authority and compassion. They were no longer there to nurture and stabilize his sons.

No father or other authority figure. Mephibosheth grew up in hiding because all the other males in his family were killed by the Philistines (1 Samuel 31). It appeared that his life would also be in danger. The entire patriarchal line had been destroyed. Mephibosheth lost his covering and became a fearful young man. He was also "lame in both feet because when he was five years old, when the news about Saul [his grandfather] and Jonathan [his father] came from Jezreel...he fell and became disabled" (2 Samuel 4:4).

Mephibosheth's handicap defined him. In his mind, he was not a son, grandson or a prince. He was simply "the lame one." I believe the community saw him that way too. Eventually their image helped to shape his self concept. When King David finally summoned him, he asked, "What is your servant, that you should notice a dead dog like me?" (2 Samuel 9:8). He felt unworthy to be in the presence of a king. He believed he had no value.

Mephibosheth came from King Saul's lineage. His father was not around to help him break the generational curse of low self esteem. Fear governed his entire existence. It was through King David's kindness that breakthrough began. He was no longer rejected, but rather reconnected to his father by the stories David recounted. That affirmation was important. It cancelled the cycle of abandonment.

Abandonment. Another Old Testament patriarch whose offspring struggled with abandonment issues was Abraham. He felt he had no choice but to exile Hagar and their son, Ishmael. His wife (Sarah) was displeased that her former servant had given birth to his son. Although Abraham initially provided for the boy, the thing most needed (his presence; his fatherly protection, guidance and nurturing) was not a part of Ishmael's life. This created a void which would eventually become filled with fear and anger. Abraham's abandonment birthed fear of further neglect, so Ishmael was perpetually on the offensive. He would attack, he would fight; he would protect himself.

God sent an angel to tell his mother that he would "be a wild donkey of a man, and that his hand would be against everyone and everyone's hand against him; that he would live in hostility towards all his brothers" (Genesis 16:11-12). God understood the dynamics of maneuvering through the fog of an unrequited desire for connection. He knew what it would do to Ishmael's emotions and psyche; after all it was He who gave us the innate longing for relationship. He designed the family nucleus. In spite of the circumstances, Ishmael longed for his natural father. Anger covered that longing and deflected the pain.

Anxiety caused by fear of abandonment creates a mask of anger. This mask causes the individual to appear strong because of its explosive nature. It is really a house for inadequacies—unspoken, hidden weaknesses. They maintain a façade which deflects further harm. If a lion began roaring as soon as he heard your approach, you would be prone to retreat. If you knew the lion had a debilitating wound and could not launch an attack, you would call the bluff and approach. In this case the lion (Ishmael) never exposed his wound, but its presence governed his life. Ishmael never conquered his fear.

Conquering Fear

To conquer fear, you must first detect it. Sometimes it is difficult to acknowledge that you allow it to control you. This denial lets it masquerade as something else. Do not let that happen. Call it what it is so that the proper tools may be used to kill it. Once fear is identified, there are three major weapons that can be used against it. They are praise, prayer and the Word of God.

Fear cannot reside in praise. It cannot withstand the power of prayer. It will always be conquered by persistent decrees and declarations of God's Word. Don't allow it access. Instead, rise up, stand up and speak out until it is vanquished.

Praise conquers fear. Praise defeats fear effortlessly. It is a weapon the devil cannot fight against. The sound of your praise calls Angels to action. Use it often. It breaks chains that seek to bind, and sets captives free. Praise in the mouth of a Saint is like an army tank against a BB gun. It outguns the enemy.

King Jehoshaphat used praise in his battle against Ammon, Moab and Mount Seir. Praise went out in front of the army, and the enemy turned on each other (2 Chronicles 20:20-22). Victory manifested as they began to sing. Get your praise on now. It crushes fear into oblivion and elevates your spirit. Enemies will be swiftly and soundly defeated.

Prayer dispels fear. Conversations with God move Heaven. Principalities and powers know they cannot stand against the prayers of a Saint. Jesus could have been afraid in the Garden of Gethsemane, but a commitment to prayer kept his spirit in a place of assurance (Matthew 26:36-46).

When Job lost everything, his conversations with God kept fear at bay, even when he spoke in error. He faltered and lost faith, only when he stopped saying what God said. As he started speaking the Word again, fear fled. Those words began a turnaround in Job's circumstances. He shook fear and embraced faith (Job 42:1-6).

The Word annihilates fear. Speak words that eliminate fear. Change perspective. Use your mouth to alter life's course. In Daniel 3, King Nebuchadnezzar tried to intimidate the three Hebrew boys by saying words he thought would make them fearful (Daniel 3:19-20). Shadrach, Meshach and Abednego boldly spoke courageous words of faith to the King (Daniel 3:16-18).

They were not afraid. His initial edict did not shake them; instead he lost control while they stood with calm assurance. Fear cannot stand against the Word of God in your mouth.

Fear seeks to control others. It dominates an individual; then tries to infect someone else through them. King Nebuchadnezzar was afraid. What would everyone in the Kingdom think if those boys did not bow to his graven image? How would those he ruled view him if he appeared soft? Mostly, he was afraid that if he let them live they would prove that his gods were powerless.

God's might was seen when he miraculously freed Shadrach, Meshach and Abednego in the midst of the fire. Fear disappeared and was replaced with wonder (Daniel 3:24-25). What happens next is inspiring.

Fear recognizes the power of faith. When King Nebuchadnezzar saw their faith and the power of God, his own fear fled. He acknowledged the Lord, and issued a decree praising Him. He then promoted Shadrach, Meshach and Abednego (Daniel 3:28-30). Fear bowed in the face of their faith. Again, fear and faith cannot coexist. One invariably displaces the other.

If you are living with a spirit of fear, begin to speak the things that are not as though they were. According to Romans 4:17, you have power to "call into being things that [are] not." Speak into the atmosphere until that which you speak manifests.

Elijah said boldly to King Ahab, "there will be neither dew nor rain in the next few years except at my word" (1 Kings 17:1) because he knew this power of faith. There was no rain until he decreed it (1 Kings 18:41). You might say, "Elijah was a prophet and I am not." Remember, you are made in the image of God (Genesis 1:27). Open your mouth and say what God has said.

Love conquers fear. "There is no fear in love...perfect love drives out fear, because fear has to do with punishment. The one who fears is not made perfect in love" (1 John 4:18). God is perfect love. Trusting Him and appropriating His Word in your life will cause fear to flee (Hebrews 4:12).

Jesus courageously offered Himself as the supreme sacrifice because of His love for humanity. He did not have to do it, but He did (John 15:13). Conversely, the love the Apostles had for Christ caused them to display the same courage. They spread the gospel fearlessly. Many died for the cause of Christ. Paul speaks of his experience in 2 Corinthians 11. In his case, courage conceived self sacrifice and declared triumphantly, above all else, love prevails. Be careful though, because that same courage can be thwarted by a spirit of offense. It is vital that you guard your mind and heart against it.

Offense

The spirit of offense is dangerous. After Jesus was arrested in the Garden, Peter was offended and afraid when someone identified him as His follower. "Peter said unto him [Jesus], Although all should be offended, yet will not I" (Mark 14:29, KJV). Still he allowed the accusation to strike fear in his heart and fear caused him to deny Jesus three times. I believe Peter's fear started when he saw Jesus praying in the Garden. There was a sense of trepidation, knowing that something was terribly wrong, yet not having any idea when all hell would break loose. When Peter saw how many soldiers were sent to arrest just one man, he became even more fearful. He watched what they did to Jesus as they led Him through the streets, and his fear magnified until it consumed him.

Judas was another person close to Jesus, who allowed a

spirit of offense to control and dictate his choices. He carried the money bag and wanted to have the final say in all financial decisions. This desire developed a renegade mindset in Judas. As he watched the activity surrounding Jesus and the reaction of the leaders to Him, he felt it was only a matter of time before Jesus was in custody.

Judas did not want to be perceived as a follower of Christ. He wanted to be known as the one who had done what seemed right in the eyes of man. Judas was full of himself, driven by flesh and more concerned about his image. He tried to secure what he thought was his future by betraying Jesus, but instead, his future lost its light.

In both situations the reactions fueled by offense ultimately caused shame. In Peter's case he was repentant and found grace. That shame caused Judas to take his own life.

Proverbs 19:11 says that, "A man's wisdom gives him patience; it is to his glory to overlook an offense." Not living in offense safeguards against wrong responses and fractured relationships. Peter and Judas lacked faith that God would preserve and protect them. They allowed fear to triumph by conquering them. Hold on to your faith. It trumps fear every time.

Lack of Faith

A lack of faith keeps you from all that is possible. Abraham and Sarah did not immediately understand this. It was only after they tried working things out themselves and made a mess (Sarah sent Abraham in to her handmaid, Hagar, and Ishmael was conceived) that they got it. Their inability to keep the faith birthed a vow of perpetual contention from a son (Ishmael) who grew up without his father. He was a casualty, conceived because they were driven by fear.

Fear creates unrest and introduces distress. It is a popular tool in the devil's arsenal. He propels it like a projectile, a fiery dart—a missile armed for maximum impact. He uses it like a Trojan horse, disguised as one thing, revealing its real identity only when it is too late. It serves as an invisible force field, you keep running toward the promise, but find yourself continually hitting that nameless obstruct that always hinders progress. If you feed faith, you will starve fear until it expires. Put an expiration date on it right now. Have faith in God. Fear not.

Disobedience

When God says fear not and you do anyway, there is a clear inability to obey what He has asked. No matter the reason, acting out of fear is contrary to what He commanded. If Adam and Eve believed when God said they would die if they ate from "the tree of the knowledge of good and evil," (Genesis 2: 17) they would not have disobeyed. The consequence of their disobedience still plagues us today (Romans 5:19).

When Satan questioned Eve, he purposely misled her, asking if God had really said they could not touch any tree in the garden (Genesis 3:1). By changing the script he took her mind off of what God had really said, and made her question why she wasn't allowed to eat from all the trees. This was foremost in her thoughts as she responded to his question. He confused the script in Eve's head until she began adding words God never said. Now the spirit of disobedience that governed him was on her.

There is an alternative. Trust God, and believe His Word. Rest on His assurances. He loves you so much, He sent His only Son, so that by His obedience you are made righteous (Romans, 5:19). Jesus obeyed by surrendering Himself to be executed. Had he disobeyed, He too would have been stained by sin. His purpose would have become perverted.

Abraham is a principle example of someone who had every reason to fear, yet obeyed. God asked him to sacrifice his only son (Isaac). Abraham prepared him for the slaughter, because he realized what, "To obey is better than sacrifice" (1 Samuel 15:22) meant. Do not let fear control your life or distort your view of destiny. Trust God, He has your back.

Watch out for Satan. He has tricks up his sleeve, and he wants to trap you in a cycle of defeat.

BEWARE OF THE ENEMY'S RUSE

Satan binds with contaminants. He keeps you away from fellowship with others who can positively influence your life. If allowed, he can influence your thoughts until you convince

yourself the things he's whispered are truth. He tricked Eve in
the Garden with one question (Genesis 3:4). That was all it
took for her to doubt. Doubt led to a decision which pulled her
out of fellowship with God. I have also experienced this doubt.

For years Satan held me captive with the fear of judgment.
It produced pride, offense, disobedience and the surrender to
fleshly desires. They momentarily soothed my brokenness. A
search for comfort connected me with people who caused the
broken pieces of my heart to become even more fragmented. In
one of those moments I wrote a song aptly titled *Broken Pieces*
that accurately described the state I was in.

> Broken pieces of my life
> Scattered now like grains of sand
> Broken pieces of my heart
> Drifting on the wind
> I'm lost again
> I need a place to lay my head
> To drift and dream the night away
> Broken pieces of my life
> Are here to stay
> Don't want to drown
> In my tears
> I lost myself in the dark of night
> Can't find my way
> I've lost sight
> Only the broken pieces
> Only the broken pieces
> ~ *Thea Harris*

If you are in that condition, do not become disheartened.
God loves you in spite of your mistakes. Release them to Him
and receive His unconditional love. It took a while for me to
accept that love, but it was the best decision I ever made.

The devil magnifies the broken state and superimposes
spirits of depression and hopelessness over it. He will take you
by the hand and lead you into a maze that traps and
debilitates. I am thankful God found me. He took all the tiny
pieces of my heart and put them back together. When He

showed me the finished work, I saw *me* through His eyes. He said, "Look! See? This is how I see you, and you are beautiful."

God can make you whole again. Past experiences may not disappear, but they don't have the same effect on you. You develop compassion for the person you were, the one that did not know love and made mistakes as a result. You walk in gratitude for God's mercy and grace. His amazing love transforms your life. Ask Him to use you to help others who face the same battles you have already overcome, and humbly worship throughout the process.

REMOVE THE CONTAMINANTS

To contaminate means, "To soil, stain, corrupt, or infect by contact or association; to make inferior or impure by admixture; or to make unfit for use by the introduction of unwholesome or undesirable elements." Contaminants infect your soul. They weigh you down with emotional sludge you cannot wade through. They mix with pure thoughts and your mind begins producing tainted thought processes. They create emotions that hold you hostage. You are controlled, a prisoner to your own mind, will and emotions.

A contaminated soul is not free to worship. It can produce a desire to be inhabited by the Spirit of God, but there are strong impediments. Feelings of unworthiness and an inability to believe that God would dwell in such an undeserving vessel, is one obstacle. Memories of past mistakes invade, just when you decide to allow the presence of God inside. The heart closes abruptly. An opportunity to experience His pure love is lost.

He provides effective tools to remove contaminants. These tools include the Word, prayer, the blood, and the name of Jesus. They infuse you with the Holy Spirit and give power to overcome, but they only work if used consistently.

EQUIPPING TOOLS

God knows the kind of enemies you will face as a Saint. He considered the weapons you would need to defeat those enemies. He has given His Word, which is "more powerful than a two-edged sword" (Hebrews 4:12). You can speak with Him at any time (Philippians 4:6).

Jesus' blood gives you power over death, the grave and every enemy (Exodus 12:13). His name commands reverence (Romans 14:11). He sent the Holy Spirit as your comforter (John 14:26). You are positioned to subdue and have dominion.

The Word

Hide the Word in your heart to keep from sinning (Psalm 119:11). "Be transformed by the renewing of your mind" (Romans 12:2). God's Word will produce life changing results. If you resist Him, when you finally acquiesce, there are varying degrees of pressure needed to break through the layers you have allowed to compound your life. As a result, the water of the Word comes as a flood or as a storm. It can also come as fire, a trickle; or it may present itself as a peaceful stream. The Word comes to the degree that it is required.

The Word as a flood. The flood covers and destroys everything in its path. It comes if you adamantly refuse to change. In the days of Noah, the flood was necessary because the people would not repent. They persisted in wrong doing until the door of the Ark was shut and rain began to fall. Those who are in this category often find their lives upside down before they surrender and settle into a new lifestyle of worship and devotion. It is important not to become alarmed if this flood hits you. This is a necessary part of the process so you can eventually move forward without self imposed barriers.

Water (Word) immersion compels spiritual renovation. The Word will renew and transform, but only if it is heard and appropriated. Your spiritual ears have to be open for sounds and frequencies that bring change. The Word makes adjustments that propel you to new dimensions. Under water, "Sound travels 4.3 times faster than in air"[2] so the water of the Word will come to you quickly. It can be more difficult to hear because of its speed.

"When the outer portion of the ears fill up with water, the eardrums can't vibrate."[2] This means that when the water of the Word comes, it is not the natural ear which is most important. It is the understanding, the receptiveness and the frequency spiritual ears are attuned to which will determine how much the Word accomplishes, and how it manifests in your life.

The components that make sound possible under water are bone, vibration and frequency. "Sound is communicated via bone conductivity in water. Sound creates vibrations, which compress the bony case in the inner ear and stimulate sensory cells that perceive sound waves. High pitched sounds cause segments of the skull to vibrate individually, while low pitched sounds vibrate the entire skull."[2]

Good vibrations are produced when an individual who absorbs the Word finds the right frequency. These vibrations bring transformation. If everything needs to be shaken, a low-frequency position will produce desired results. High frequencies are necessary when someone has already been in the change process for some time and specific areas require strategic targeting. [4] It is possible to hear accurately in the flood; but it is also vitally important to be on the right frequency and have your spiritual ears honed for messages that will transform.

Bone function is also critical. Bones house the marrow which contains cells that are vital for survival. Without the marrow, there is no life. "Bone marrow cells carry oxygen to the tissues; platelets in the marrow prevent bleeding and aid in the clotting of blood, and lymphocytes in the marrow kill or isolate invading cells and myeloid cells which fight infections, remove dead cells and remodel tissue and bones."[3] The Word of God is the container, the defense, the source of life, the purge. It acts as spiritual marrow, serving your mind, heart and spirit. It prevents you from becoming a casualty in the war against Satan, placing you in a position to consistently rule.

Just like contaminated marrow requires a transfusion so that the individual will become healthy again, the Word is a spiritual transfusion bringing renewal. Go directly to the source. Ask God to download revelation.

The path to cleansing is sometimes littered with words, persons and situations that try to keep you dirty. It is important to have an accurate Word. Sanctify yourself. Hebrews 4:12 refers to the Word of God as "living and active, sharper than any two-edged sword, piercing to the division of soul and of spirit, of joints and of marrow, and discerning the thoughts and intentions of the heart" (ESV). Ezekiel used the Word to bring dead bones to life. He testifies,

> The hand of the Lord was upon me, and he brought me out in the Spirit of the Lord and set me down in the middle of the valley; it was full of bones. And he led me around among them, and behold, there were very many on the surface of the valley, and behold, they were very dry. And he said to me, "Son of man, can these bones live?" And I answered, "O Lord God, you know." Then he said to me, "Prophesy over these bones, and say to them, O dry bones, hear the word of the Lord. Thus says the Lord God to these bones: Behold, I will cause breath to enter you, and you shall live (Ezekiel 37:1-5).

The high frequency of Ezekiel's sound rattled those bones, and created vibrations which brought new life.

Vibration frequency needs to be precise. Too much vibration can cause great harm, like strong earthquakes. You must be sensitive about how much is needed, and where it is needed to avoid unnecessary damage. Managing frequency levels minimizes this concern. If your frequency is out of sorts, the Word can minimize negative vibrations and help maintain spiritual equilibrium.

The Word as the storm. Great offenses that are often repeated (although you know they are wrong), self-destructive behavior, and sexual sins draw raging storms that affect contaminated areas. The storm swirls, shakes, rattles, and breaks off unhealthy attachments. It humbles until there is a yielding.

King David encountered many storms. One of the most memorable was the outcome of his sin with Bathsheba (2 Samuel 11). David secretly watched her bathing on the roof. He lusted after her in his heart. That lust directed his thoughts and eventually his thoughts created desires which encompassed him. He compromised his relationship with God. He compromised Bathsheba and her relationship with her husband.

David abused his power as King when he summoned her to his bed. Her husband was on the battlefield fighting a battle that David should have been fighting as well. His sin happened because he was out of position. It evolved to greater evil as David sought to keep it hidden.

When Bathsheba sent a message about her pregnancy to David, he knew the child was his and had her husband (Uriah) murdered. David's offenses progressed from one level of depravity to another. He was not accountable to anyone. He did not seek help before a look escalated to adultery, then murder.

After Uriah died, "David had her [Bathsheba] brought to his house, and she became his wife and bore him a son. But the thing David had done displeased the LORD" (2 Samuel 11:27). The storm began swirling in David's life and God sent a prophet (Nathan) to confront him (2 Samuel 12:1-7).

David lost sight of the gravity of his sin. Nathan's revelation was a strong force to his spirit but it was only after Nathan said it that David acknowledged wrongdoing. Hidden sins anesthetize the conscience and offenses are repeated with no conviction. This eventually escalates to a spiritual condition where there is persistence in wrong doing. The consequences of sin affected many in David's life. It is important to walk uprightly, especially if your anointing has the ability to destroy others.

Those closest to you suffer the results of storms you draw because of hidden sin. Bathsheba lost a husband, and a son because of David's sinful acts. He was a man after God's heart, with a strong anointing, so his dishonor produced severe results. Read further in the chapter. His children were born into the stain of his secret sin. They would suffer the consequences as well. David's transgressions were too great. God forgave him, but the price of his actions rippled into his family's future.

Your attitude in the storm determines how long you are in it. David knew the importance of worshipping in the storm. While he was suffering the consequences of his actions, he worshipped. The storm did not change his perspective. He knew God was just and faithful. He did not pray for Him to remove the storm; he understood the reason for it.

He was willing to accept whatever chastisement was meted out. He acknowledged wrongdoing and allowed the scourging to transform his mind and spirit. David prayed,

> Have mercy on me, O God, according to your unfailing love; according to your great compassion blot out my transgressions. Wash away all my iniquity and cleanse me from my sin. For I know my transgressions, and my sin is always before me. Against you, you only, have I sinned and done what is evil in your sight; so you are right in your verdict and justified when you judge (Psalm 51:1-4).

There was a reward for this humble posture. After the storm David was blessed with a son (Solomon) who acquired great wealth. He had a reputation as one of the wisest men in Israel and was anointed to build God's Tabernacle. Solomon had great renown. He was respected by many and his service was a part of God's plan to restore the children of Israel and initiate a greater level of worship.

The Word as fire. The fiery Word exposes hidden things and introduces them to a process of purification until there is freedom and complete cleansing. In Jeremiah 23:29, God asks, "Is not my word like fire." If you are yielded to the Holy Spirit in the purification process, the fire will consume only that which contaminates you. It also warms that which has gone cold (2 Timothy 1:6).

When you read the Word, the flame is fanned. It is also fanned by men and women of God with accurate prophecy. Do not be afraid to let the Word work. It is from God and will bear witness in your spirit. Be mindful, not everyone who operates in the gift of prophecy speaks accurately. The gift without the anointing is perverted. Ask God to sharpen your discernment so you cannot be deceived.

The Word as a trickle. Sometimes you are in fellowship with God, but allow sin access. It finds a place deep inside your spirit and rests there. If you are not careful, it locates spiritual fractures and lodges so deeply, the water of the Word washes over them. This is possible when you have not identified transgressions or offered them unto the Lord. These little foxes are overlooked. They need a potent trickle from the main water source to seep in and form a stream that eventually dislodges them. They must be loosened so they are easily washed away when the Word is reapplied (Proverbs 6:16-19).

The Word as a peaceful stream. Although God chastens those He loves, He does not abandon them in the chastening. You are not alone when the storm comes to transform. Jesus is right there and you can call to Him in the storm. He will soothe your spirit. In Psalm 23:2 David spoke of the Lord, his shepherd, provider, protector, and comforter saying, "He lets me rest in green meadows; he leads me beside peaceful streams" (NLT). God may afflict the flesh to propel you toward destiny and purpose, but as the soul is being scourged, he provides relief.

If you get the Word but never appropriate it, the enemy will attack. After the Word has touched your spirit, let it become active so you can grow. It must move in and through your life to allow permanent change to happen.

My husband works on boats, and sometimes when they are brought in there are barnacles on the bottom and hull (below the waterline) of the vessel. Barnacles are "marine crustaceans that, are covered with a shell made of hard calcium-containing plates and are permanently cemented, head down, to rocks, pilings, ships' hulls." They attach themselves because the boat has been sitting in water for an extended period without movement.

If you don't use the Word, it calcifies like the barnacles on a stagnant boat. The non-working Word fuses with a contrary spirit that keeps it trapped. When it is trapped, you are full of Word with no nourishment or transformation.

The enemy superimposes himself over a dormant word. Although a portion of the boat's hull is surrounded by water, when the vessel sits for a prolonged period, barnacles gel with the surface. They become a part of it and serious work is required to remove them before any repairs, painting or polishing can be done to the affected area. In other words, for that area to be brand new again, careful labor intensive scraping is necessary.

Some vessels are so bad they need sustained sandblasting (using compressed air to blast sand with great speed and force) to remove the barnacles. The process of removal is painstaking and time consuming. Like vessels that need sandblasting, you need a powerful, piercing, sustained application of the Word to undo damage. Let it work in you.

Collateral Damage
While God was still downloading the full concepts to be covered in this book, I had a dream. I was in a bathroom with white shower tiles. The ones on the bottom were almost completely covered with grime. They were a filthy dark green and black in some areas. I was holding a water hose on the tiles, thinking, I need more than water to get these clean. When the water hit them, the grime started falling away. They literally peeled off like scabs, fell to the shower floor, and completely disintegrated. Some tiles required that I hold the hose on them for a longer period, moving the water back and forth until the filth was gone.

The tiles the water cleaned were sparkling – brand new, as if they were newly installed. The white was vivid as if grime had never touched them.

There were also some tiles on the top right corner that wouldn't become clean. Although they were not as filthy as the grime covered tiles, I had to hold the hose in the seam where they connected with the wall and give it sustained water pressure. Eventually, those tiles came away with a huge chunk of the wall still attached to them. The work was arduous.

Destroying deeply entrenched pollutants means eliminating areas that have festered. Contaminants though not visible, are doing serious damage. If a life threatening infection is allowed to multiply in the body without treatment; death is imminent. During an operation, doctors may find an infection has spread to surrounding tissue. To save the life of the patient, that tissue must be removed as well.

Your spirit suffers the same fate when you cannot submit

to the washing of the Word. It comes, but there is no cleansing. Pride pushes it into the recesses of your soul. There need not be collateral damage, but it can only be avoided if you surrender as the Word identifies areas which must be cleaned.

It washes easily, if you yield completely to God's dealings in your life. If you are heavily contaminated, sustained application of the Word is vital. When you resist, cleansing is prolonged and a deep rooting out of contaminants follows. This is often a more painful process.

Yielding means you can be cleansed and nourished. Opposition to the process assures a scourging. Whether the Word comes as a flood, a storm or a trickle, it can and will remove contaminants. God wants you. He needs you to rise in stature and declare His works as you draw others into the Kingdom. He is in the midst as you endure.

Once the Word removes contaminants from your heart, you are able to launch its power against the enemy. Jesus used it in the wilderness, and Satan could not withstand the Word. He fled and Angels on assignment came and ministered to Jesus (Matthew 4:1-11).

A swimmer caught in a tidal wave is advised not to fight the current, but to swim with it. In other words, cooperate with the water until they are safely out of the current. Fighting against the water means physical death is probable. So it is in the realm of the spirit, and if you fight against the washing of the Word, spiritual death will occur. Submit to cleansing for healing and growth.

The Word works—both to wash and to equip you for Kingdom purpose. When it comes, keep your eyes on Jesus. He is always there. Whatever you do, do not abort your process. Sometimes as the Word is working, it feels like you are drowning. You become seasick, lose hope, develop fears, and your faith fails.

You can't give up. Stay plugged in. Keep reading, meditating and studying until you become that Word. "Say with confidence, the Lord is my helper, I will not be afraid" (Hebrews 13:6). The Word is life and truth. If you allow it to saturate you, it will touch every area that needs change (John 7:37-38).

Prayer: Power & Accuracy

As you are being washed by the Word, you will find decay or contaminants that require a combination of the Word and prayer. Only the Holy Spirit can restore the sections of your soul that are already in a state of decomposition. He can reach into the depths of your spirit with surgical precision and excise that which is impeding movement. Go to Him in prayer. It is a commanding tool that pricks the ears of God, and touches His heart. Suit up, engage the right enemy, fight the right battle, and pray (Ephesians 6:10-18).

Warfare begins and ends in the spirit realm. When you pray, angels go to war for you. Ephesians six speaks of "spiritual forces of evil in the heavenly realms" (vs. 12). Daniel had to wait twenty-one days while the host of heaven battled on his behalf (Daniel 10). I often wonder what would have happened if he became discouraged and stopped praying. "Pray without ceasing" (I Thessalonians 5:17).

Angels will fight for you. Do not give up; your prayers have been heard and are being answered right now. Bathe the heavens, secure spiritual territory, replenish your arsenal and wait for the manifestation (2 Corinthians 10:3-6). There is nothing God cannot deliver you from; there is no hurt He cannot heal.

Too often people think of prayer as one sided, but God is longing to speak. If your relationship with Him is fractured, repair it so you can experience His manifest power. You must arm yourself, wield power and be accurate with your weaponry. You have authority. Be deliberate in your prayer time. An archer may hit the enemy from a great distance, but if he is not accurate, he will only wound him. Be skillful; you are equipped to destroy the enemy (Luke 10:17-19).

Worship generates greater power in your prayer life. The relationship between Jesus and the seventy-two individuals He sent out to serve the people gave them a measure of power that caused demons to submit; not in their own strength, but in the name of the Lord (Luke 10:1-3). He sent them as lambs among wolves. He knew they could navigate any environment. The power contained everything needed to transform all atmospheres. It was Kingdom power (Luke 10:11).

The prophet Elijah understood the correlation between worship, relationship and a manifestation of Kingdom power (I Kings 18:32). He built an altar before he called down fire from Heaven. His task required the full power of God's Presence which always manifests in worship. The prophets of Baal were defeated because Elijah assumed a posture of reverence and acknowledgment of his Sovereign King.

Pour the water (Word) over your worship. Saturate it until God comes. Elijah instructed, fill "Four barrels with water, and pour it on the burnt sacrifice, and on the wood. And he said, Do it the second time. And they did it the second time. And he said, Do it the third time. And they did it the third time. And the water ran round about the altar" (I Kings 18:33-35, KJV). Water surrounded the sacrifice. Four barrels were poured three times. This is significant. Twelve is the number of spiritual government.

Only after this saturation did Elijah pray, "Hear me, O Lord, hear me, that this people may know that thou art the Lord God, and that thou hast turned their heart back again. The fire of the Lord fell, and consumed the burnt sacrifice, and the wood, and the stones, and the dust, and licked up the water that was in the trench. And when all the people saw it, they fell on their faces: and they said, The Lord, he is the God; the Lord, he is the God" (I Kings 18:37-39, KJV). As a result of this move, Baal worshippers captured and destroyed their own prophets (1 Kings 18:39-40). The power was drawn in prayer, through worship.

A governmental anointing is activated by the Word. Whenever God initiated governmental moves in the earth, the number twelve appeared. There were twelve tribes to govern Israel (Genesis 49). He made a covenant with Israel and called Moses up to the mount with the elders. After Moses worshipped, he built twelve pillars to represent the tribes of Israel. He established the covenant and then spoke as God instructed (Exodus 24:1-18).

When God told Israel to take possession of the promise

land, they sent out twelve spies to get information to develop strategic warfare tactics (Deuteronomy 1). Once the children of Israel crossed over the Jordan, twelve men were chosen to facilitate the transition process. After the crossing, they used twelve stones to build a memorial. It was a reminder that the Presence of God had removed obstacles and made a way to gain access to what He promised (Joshua 3:11-13). God's people purified themselves and experienced His Presence. This cleared the path to a triumphant future (Joshua 4:1-7).

The righteous are protected in worship. It commissions the government of Heaven to defend the Saint. Exodus thirty-nine speaks of a cloak of righteousness, the breastplate, which was made like an ephod (a garment of worship) and adorned in jewels. There were four rows, each containing three precious stones. The twelve stones represented the twelve tribes of Israel (vs. 8-14). The breastplate shields and deflects attacks when necessary.

You cannot have the governmental anointing without purification and worship. Position yourself to receive blessings that are drawn to that anointing. Demons will run at the sound of your voice. You are able to call "things that be not as though they were" (Romans 4:17, KJV).

Your worship and prayer draws the power into your life until it becomes a testimony, a catalyst which presents hope to those whose lives you are called to impact. It compels the reverent and receptive to become converted. They willingly offer themselves to be used in the Kingdom.

Prayer increases the capacity to handle intense storms. Jesus understood the power of prayer. He always went away to solitary places, to talk to God (Luke 5:16, Mark 1:35). He talked to His Father before making important decisions (Luke 6:12-13). He consulted Him when he was faced with difficult challenges (Matthew 26:36-44). His prayer times were not relegated to times of pressure. He knew everything in His life and ministry relied on that connection. He prayed to be in constant communion as He lived in purpose (John 17:25). Jesus prayed for the glory to manifest before the people, that they might see God's power and experience His love. He prayed they would understand the value in His sacrifice (John 17:1-3).

Christ's prayer life was not only for Him (Romans 8:34). Each time He went before God, someone benefited, even in Gethsemane. He prayed for strength, but it was not a selfish prayer. He needed grace to die so you might be free. Jesus knew that His relationship with God would ensure man's redemption, and He set the example.

Prayer keeps you focused. Jesus did not glory in His accomplishments. He needed God so that virtue would be restored continually. It was not about notoriety for Him, and it should not be for you either.

Acknowledging God as your source enhances the anointing on your life. Jesus knew it was critical to stay plugged into the Power. That's why miracles, signs and wonders followed Him. He healed the sick, raised the dead, and walked on water (Mark 6:48-50). Nothing was impossible because He had no doubt or fear. Jesus never underestimated the Power.

A Praying Spirit

Ask God for a spirit of prayer. Stay in His presence until a level of spiritual authority develops. Daniel's prayer life kept God's power active throughout his captivity in Babylon. Because of his praying spirit, he was humble, trustworthy, uncorrupted, obedient, insightful and consistent. It amplified his anointing and caused him to develop a covenant heart.

Daniel had the spirit of an armor bearer, and honored those who ruled over him. This increased his wisdom, knowledge and understanding. The mysteries of heaven were revealed to him. He walked in a powerful spiritual dimension which drew prevailing angels to his aide as he prayed.

Every demand he made on Heaven received an immediate response. If you develop the same level of intimacy with God, nothing will be withheld from you (Psalm 84:11). It is Christ's shed blood that endows you with this prevailing power.

The Blood

Every major organ in your body is sustained by blood. Your physical body needs it to survive. Jesus' blood guarantees eternal life. He was "slain to receive power and wealth and wisdom and strength and honor and glory and praise" (Revelation 5:12). He died so you could overcome. He took your penalty so you might be free. His blood triumphs in you each day as you serve. It secured atonement for your sins and it conquered death. You can have great joy at the prospect of abundant life (Hebrews 9:22, KJV).

Christ's death "redeemed you from the curse of the law" (Galatians 3:13). "He was wounded for your transgressions; he was bruised for your iniquities" (Isaiah 53:5). His blood stained the path to the cross and the cross itself. Surrender to God; follow Christ; Embrace the power. The Apostle Paul, speaking to the Ephesians, spoke of this power as he sought to establish an understanding of Kingdom authority (Ephesians 1:18-23).

The blood reconciles you to God. When Jesus gave up His life, His purpose was fulfilled. It was no longer necessary for a Priest to go to God on man's behalf. You have direct access to God (Romans 8:15). The blood provides entrance to the Holy Place where you can encounter Him. It opens dimensions where He intimately shares with you.

In the Old Testament, after the priests presented the blood offering – they prepared themselves to enter into the Holy of Holies through a process of purification. A blood offering was required to purify the altar; and to purify their worship. They atoned for the people. How wonderful to know that Christ became the blood offering (Romans 5:8-10). He paid the price to atone for your sin—what a wonderful gift.

The blood and covenant. In the Old Testament days, a male bullock was killed. The blood was sprinkled upon the altar by the door of the Tabernacle to prepare to offer a pure sacrifice unto the Lord (Leviticus 1:1-11). The blood was the sign of covenant. God is a covenant God. He promised to send a deliverer to save mankind. He did not lie (Numbers 23:19). He sent Jesus whose blood was shed to fulfill the covenant. When He died your redemption was sealed. His blood secured new life. If you believe Him and accept Him as your Savior, you can be saved.

The blood and protection. When God decreed He would strike the firstborns of Egypt, He commanded the children of Israel to apply blood to their door posts (Exodus 12:12 -13). Marked households were spared because of the blood. Apostle Paul said, "He forgave us all our sins, having canceled the charge of our legal indebtedness, which stood against us and condemned us; he has taken it away, nailing it to the cross. And having disarmed the powers and authorities, he made a public spectacle of them, triumphing over them by the cross" (Colossians 2:13-15). Protection was sure because of Jesus' shed blood. There is also power in His name.

The Name of Jesus
The name of Jesus is a weapon. Speak it in humility and with resolve. Blind Bartimaeus could not see, but he understood the power of the name. He shouted repeatedly, "Jesus, Son of David, have mercy on me" (Mark 10:47). He called until Jesus heard and was spurred to action. A blind beggar moved Heaven with an insistent call upon the name.

Demons tremble at the name. The man with the unclean spirit in the country of the Gedarenes was bound because he was wild, untamable (Mark 5:4). Chains could not restrain him. When he recognized Jesus, his loud cry initiated deliverance (Mark 4:7). Heaven moved for him like it had for blind Bartimaeus. Speaking the name commanded spirits that possessed him to come out. Those spirits also spoke the name, not understanding that evil spirits cannot access that power. It brought them no deliverance. Rather, their fears were exposed. They had to acknowledge the power Jesus' name wields.

The name of the Lord Jesus Christ is above all others (Philippians 2:8-11). Its power is unparalleled, but your heart must be completely surrendered to access it. If pride is present, you contribute to your downfall. Stay humble. Humility is an important component which releases the power.

Humility
Humility prepares your heart for transformation. A heart that

is not humble has no capacity to secure spiritual weaponry, and therefore no ability to withstand the devil's attacks. Do not get lifted in pride. A humble heart is willing to receive instruction from God. It surrenders to His will, and can be trusted to execute His plans. In this state, your mind and emotions will not hinder God's move in your life.

Samson became proud, stubborn and foolish. His anointing constantly fueled his strength, but the accolades he received caused humility to slowly dissipate until he was only doing what he wanted. Samson exposed his anointing to the enemy and became weak, ineffective, blind and imprisoned. It wasn't until after he became humble again that God re-fueled and re-fired him. He brought down the Philistines as had been purposed to do from birth. The Bible says "those who exalt themselves will be humbled, and those who humble themselves will be exalted" (Matthew 26:12).

Without the anointing Samson was powerless to accomplish great feats in the name of the Lord. With it, he exhibited supernatural courage and strength. Like Samson, you are apt to wind up walking paths that lead you into destruction. Without the Holy Spirit you have no power.

Your Unseen Partner: The Holy Spirit
After His resurrection, Jesus told the disciples, "And now I will send the Holy Spirit, just as my Father promised. But stay here in the city until the Holy Spirit comes and fills you with power from heaven" (Luke 24:49). There was a fulfillment of His promise in Acts two. They obeyed His command, and The Holy Spirit came with demonstrated power.

After He touched them, they became emboldened. Peter's message of Christ's death, resurrection and the gift of the Holy Spirit caused "about three thousand souls to be added" (Acts 2:29-41) to the Kingdom.

"Tongues of fire rested on the disciples" (Acts 2:3). This fire was symbolic. It was a call to greater manifestations of the authority and sovereignty of God. Man became the recipient and the transmitter of the power and favor of God. Endowed with grace, they fulfilled purpose (Acts 2:1-21). Miracles, signs and wonders followed throughout the nations as they proclaimed the gospel.

Moses had a similar experience. His call to deliver the children of Israel was initiated by an encounter that started with fire in a bush. It was a fire that did not consume, but instead demonstrated the power of God. There was an Angel with instructions and equipping power for Moses (Exodus 3:3-10). With that Power, an entire nation was delivered out of the hands of a tyrant King. They also saw signs, miracles and wonders. Although Moses initially thought himself unworthy, purpose manifested.

To receive the power of the Holy Spirit, all contaminants must be eradicated. He will not reside in mess. Make yourself a habitation, a place where He can dwell continually. He will comfort, guide and teach you. He will equip you to thwart every plot of the enemy and wreck havoc on the forces of darkness. He will prepare you for destiny (John 14:26). Arm yourself for the spiritual battle. Advance and defend with courage.

ARM YOURSELF

Your armor has your name on it. Put it on. Not just some of it, but all of it. Every uncovered area is vulnerable to attack. It gives Satan a foothold on ground his feet should not touch. Arm yourself by putting on "The full armor of God, so that when the day of evil comes, you may be able to stand your ground. Stand firm then, with the belt of truth buckled around your waist, with the breastplate of righteousness in place, and with your feet fitted with the readiness that comes from the gospel of peace.

In addition to all this, take up the shield of faith, with which you can extinguish all the flaming arrows of the evil one. Take the helmet of salvation and the sword of the Spirit, which is the word of God" (Ephesians 6:13-17). Gird yourself with truth, righteousness, peace, faith, salvation and God's Word. What better way to annihilate a spiritual foe than to drape yourself in this armament? Adorn yourself to fight and win!

Another way to be sure you are fully protected is to feed on and become entrenched by the fruit of the spirit. These are weapons that will wound the enemy without hurting people.

"The fruit of the spirit is love, joy, peace, forbearance, kindness, goodness, faithfulness, gentleness and self-control. Against such things there is no law" (Galatians 5:22-23). The devil cannot use these weapons, but if you put them on, it will keep him bound. Remember, "the weapons of your warfare are not carnal but mighty through God to the pulling down of strongholds" (2 Corinthians 10:4, KJV).

Now you are ready. You will conquer and maintain true life by accurately arming yourself to engage the enemy in a battle whose outcome is already in your favor. Individuals with contaminated spirits have difficulty wearing this armor. Submit to the process of purification and nothing can hinder Kingdom progress.

BATHE IN THE WATER: PURIFICATION

Have you ever watched water squirting on the windshield of your car as wipers clean the glass until you can see clearly? I once ran out of water, but did not realize it. When I turned the wiper blades on, they made a greater mess than what was already there. Without water, there was no cleansing. I could not see well.

During purification, the water of the Word opens spiritual eyes by first cleaning the mind and heart. Paul admonishes, "present your bodies a living sacrifice, holy, acceptable unto God...And be not conformed to this world: instead he asked you to be transformed by the renewing of your mind" (Romans 12:1-2, KJV).

"The brain and heart are composed of 73% water and the lungs are about 83% water. The skin contains 64% water, muscles and kidneys are 79%, and even the bones are watery: 31%. Each day humans must consume a certain amount of water to survive."[4] It is the Word (water) that helps to renew your mind daily.

Purification prepares you to receive the anointing and qualifies you to be validated by God. Allow your spirit to be washed by the Word. Surrender completely. Go through the process of sanctification to remove all contaminants (Hebrews 10:19-22).

Water exposes contaminants. All impurities may not be easily seen. When water connects with them it either draws the lighter (seemingly insignificant) pieces to the top and exposes them, or becomes dirty as it draws out impurities that exist. Some things need to be washed more than once. Thankfully, impurities do not stain the water of the Word. It cleanses but never becomes tainted.

A renewed mind transforms the soul and strengthens the spirit until it is built up and strong enough to govern consistently. In Ephesians 5:25-26, Paul says, "Christ gave Himself that He may sanctify the church with the washing of the water by the Word" (KJV). The process of purification is free. Jump into the water. Let it prepare you for the anointing.

Purity coupled with the oil safeguards those who are called. If you forego the cleansing process, yet operate under the anointing, it can destroy you. Christ is the example. He always remained pure and closely connected to His Father. All the miracles He performed would not have been possible if He was contaminated.

You can never be accurately prepared for the oil without the process. Identify contaminants. Know your enemy. Remove all impurities and allow yourself to embrace the word as fire, as scourger, as salve, as an instrument of preparation. Purpose is calling; and destiny waits.

Get ready for the oil. Become fit for the Master's use. Let the anointing fall until the power rises. Allow the Holy Spirit to reign within. If the oil saturates you, then everything and everyone you touch will become affected. Isaiah said, "Here am I, send me" (Isaiah 6:8, KJV). Will you yield? Will you go? Will you serve?

╬
Prayer
Power of God - Sovereign Father, Holy Spirit, fall right now. Cleanse and purify right now. Every fiber of my being now; I desire transformation Lord. Lord, I yield to conformation of your Word 'til flesh has died, and all that burns within is spirit.

How I yearn for your embrace. God, anoint my head with oil, causing it to flow until everything I am is covered, saturated Lord by You. Reign in me oh Holy Spirit.

Use me as you will.
In Jesus' Name - Amen.

Chapter Two

❧

ANOINTING FALL ON ME

The enemy is cunning and deceptive. He is a strategist. Often his plans to destroy you have been in play before you were born. He will do anything to disqualify every vessel worthy of the anointing. Wounds that contaminate are assigned by him, sometimes to very young children. As you persist in your move toward God's ultimate plan for your life, inevitably you must identify those wounds and seek deliverance so the enemy has no weapon that will prosper.

I have already expressed how important it is to be prepared for the anointing. What has not yet been discussed in detail is exactly how far Satan is willing to go to accomplish his purpose. He wants to trap and disempower you.

Sometimes you work your way beyond wounds to what you believe is a healthy place only to find you are dealing with the same issues over and over again. You become trapped in a cycle. You cannot find your way out of the maze. The cause of your wound might have happened at such a young age; all it left was an impression. You don't know why you are caught in the cycle; you just are. There is a nagging feeling that is never quite identified. The devil uses it to haunt you.

There is good news. God IS able, *if* you ask Him to reveal the root of the issue, you can be completely delivered. Don't allow that impression to drive your motives, responses, or decisions. Removing demonically implanted seeds is a crucial part of consecration. There is no reason why the anointing will not fall if you prepare and position yourself accurately.

Consecration

The second stanza of Fanny Crosby's hymn, "I Am Thine Oh Lord," echoes Ms. Crosby's desire to be in God's complete will. She prays, "Consecrate me now to Thy service, Lord, by the pow'r of grace divine; Let my soul look up with a steadfast hope, and my will be lost in thine." It acknowledges that the process of consecration is not possible without the power of God's grace. You need Him every step of the way to overcome diabolical obstacles that seek to destabilize purpose and lead to destruction. This can only happen if you refuse to humbly submit to the process of consecration.

Among the Levites in the Old Testament, that process was both ritualistic and regimented. It gave attention to purifying key areas that were prone to allowing contaminants to stain the spirit. The steps were specific (Leviticus 14:15-18).

God was acknowledged first, then the hands, ears, feet, and head were anointed before atonement. These areas (*hands, ears, feet, and head*) are gates that open into dimensions that will elevate, celebrate or propel you toward heavenly assignments. They can also mark you for a journey deep into the recesses of hell if you do not keep them pure. Consider pertinent reasons why hands must be kept clean at all times.

Hands. You lose spiritual dimensions when you touch things that are off limits. David touched someone else's wife (Bathsheba) and became a murderer (2 Samuel 11). Ananias and Sapphira kept money that should have been given to the Lord and died because of it (Acts 5:1-11). What about Gehazi? He became leprous after receiving gifts his master (Elisha) had refused (2 Kings 5). Samson lost his anointing because he touched Delilah, an unholy woman, a harlot who was outside his faith (Judges 16). Abraham touched Hagar. He was intimate with her at his wife's suggestion and inadvertently spawned a people that would fight against him as long as he lived (Genesis 16). Achan took spoils from the enemy and hid them in his tent after God said not to. He brought a plague on his people; and ultimately lost his life (Joshua 7). Uzzah touched the place of worship (Ark of the Covenant) inaccurately and was struck dead (1 Chronicles 13).

It is dangerous to touch things that bring dishonor to God. Be mindful of where you place your hands, and how you use them. If they connect with the right things and the right people, miracles happen.

The woman with the issue of blood whose story is chronicled in Mark five, touched Jesus' garment and was made whole after twelve years of a seemingly incurable illness. Mary touched Jesus' feet in worship and received redemption and validation before men (John 12). Jesus warned about hands that "cause us to stumble, [saying] cut it off and throw it away" (Matthew 5:30). He knew the power of the hands both for good, and evil.

Hands must be kept clean because lives depend on it. There are signs in restaurants, hospitals and bathrooms across the world, reminding people to wash their hands. Why is it that important? Hands that are infected unknowingly expose an exponential amount of people to contamination. Everything they touch becomes dirty or infected.

Contaminated hands require repeated washing to become clean again. In hospitals, the cleansing method is rigorous and precise. Personnel receive detailed instructions about how to wash. One of the methods is a timed five minute scrub. It is necessary because, according to Deborah Gardner, "the hands are the most important tools for caring and...can also be a portal and transmitter of infection."[1]

When your spirit is tainted, contaminated imprints are left on the souls of people with whom you connect. King David said, "The LORD has dealt with me according to my righteousness; according to the cleanness of my hands he has rewarded me" (Psalm 18:20). He was rewarded according to the cleanness of his hands in God's sight. Not in the sight of man, but in God's sight.

The next gate anointed by the priests was the ears, but let us talk about the eyes as well. What goes into the ears, if received, can change your visual perspective, and by extension your actions and your walk.

Ears and eyes. Several weeks ago someone came to me, very excited, and said they thought one of the married sisters in the church was having a baby. I had seen this sister, week after week yet never noticed. I am not blind, I just wasn't looking. I chided the individual, "Why are you telling me this? I don't want to know. You don't even know if it's true, yet you're saying it. I hope you're not repeating it to other people!" Yet, each time I saw the "probably pregnant" sister after that, my eyes were almost immediately (unconsciously) drawn to her stomach. Why? A gate had been opened, and once that happens, it takes a massive dose of strong will and the Holy Spirit to shut it completely. My spirit was vexed for a while, and I could not understand why I had that encounter.

I asked God about it and He said, "I had to show the powerful connection between these gates. An unsolicited statement in the ears, linked directly with the mind, and controlled the eyes each time that person appeared. I needed to show you that although you are careful, you can still be susceptible to this infection if you are not vigilant. The information was unwanted, yet the ears, mind and eyes were working in concert - all the while struggling against the heart and spirit."

Proverbs advises, "Above all else, guard your heart, for everything you do flows from it" (Proverbs 4:23). Watch your interactions. Know the spirit of the people around you. God kept reminding me how easy it is for focus to be shifted, how easy it is for wrong influence to take hold. I heard a pronouncement, and because I heard, I now saw.

If you succumb to subtle pressures your faith will be affected. You will find yourself in situations and wonder, "How did I get here?" You will be blinded to the changes occurring in your heart, until you suddenly become aware of the final destination and begin soul searching.

That is exactly what happened to Adam and Eve in the garden. Once they tasted the forbidden fruit, their spiritual eyes were opened and proved detrimental. They lost a powerful dimension in God and gained a world of pain and trouble. Satan said to Eve, "God knows that when you eat from it your eyes will be opened, and you will be like God, knowing good and evil" (Genesis 3:5). Eve listened because she wanted her eyes to be opened. She wanted to see although God had specifically said "no." Adam and Eve failed to avert their eyes from what was forbidden.

In Matthew chapter five, Jesus admonished, "If your right eye causes you to stumble, gouge it out and throw it away. It is better for you to lose one part of your body than for your whole body to be thrown into hell" (Verse 29). Be careful what you see. Job understood how important it was to protect the eye gate. He said, "I have made a covenant with my eyes not to look lustfully at another woman" (Job 31:1). The eye gate must be carefully and consistently protected. It will save you from unwanted problems.

You do not have to initiate the opening of these gates in order to be assaulted by the consequences. People can force them open, and you should fight the impulse to allow it. It is important to secure your gates with God's Word and His presence. The Bible says, "Submit yourselves, then, to God. Resist the devil and he will flee from you" (James, 4:7). Refuse to give in or he will hang around, wreak havoc and leave casualties in his path.

Run from folks who continually try to bring dimensions of evil into your life. Deflect the influence of those you cannot avoid with the Word. Keep in mind that the influencers will not always look evil or approach in a malicious manner. Some of them will be your friends. If you are not discerning, vigilantly resolving to not allow undue influence, you can be easily overcome.

Guarding your feet is as important as guarding your hands, eyes and ears.

Feet. Jesus shared a key principle in an encounter with Peter when he began to wash the feet of His disciples. Peter said, "You shall never wash my feet." Jesus answered, "Unless I wash you, you have no part with me." "Then, Lord," Simon Peter replied, "not just my feet but my hands and my head as well!" Jesus answered, "Those who have had a bath need only to wash their feet; their whole body is clean" (John 13:8-10). If your feet are clean; your whole body is clean. Profound statement!

The body needs feet to move it from one place to another. Feet can walk you into positive, prosperous places or negative, destructive places. They take you where your eyes and ears can be defiled, or where your hands have access to things they should not touch. They take you into venues where your mind is tainted or transformed. Clean feet keep you in paths that are uncontaminated and promote a chaste lifestyle (1 Peter 1:14-16).

A pure walk establishes peace and victory in battles that are waged in the mind. Keep the Word in your heart. It will direct you (Psalm 119:105). Stay on a path of righteousness so you can say like David, "He makes my feet like the feet of a deer; he causes me to stand on the heights ... and provides a broad path for my feet, so that my ankles do not give way" (Psalm 18:33, 36). It is a light that will keep you in a pure place. The enemy attacks the mind to control the narrative, thus controlling your life. Let us take a look at that.

Head. Paul repeatedly did things he had no desire to do. He wrestled daily to change his mind from old thought patterns. He wanted to end the cycle of continually committing sin. He called it a thorn in his flesh, a temptation which drove him to the cross continually. Only with the help of the Holy Spirit could he remain closely connected to God.

Paul is not the only one who had such a thorn. Peter often struggled with his mouth, sometimes speaking and acting rashly. Jesus once addressed the spirit behind his words, saying, "Get behind me, Satan! You are a stumbling block to me; you do not have in mind the concerns of God, but merely human concerns" (Matthew 16:23). Those were strong words, yet on another occasion, Peter spoke in a moment of fear, doing the unthinkable. He denied that he knew Jesus (John 18:16-27).

Everyone battles their own fleshly desires; whether it is pride, jealousy, anger, hypocrisy, gossip, backbiting, lust, or hearts that struggle to love the way that Christ loves. The mind needs to be renewed daily (James 1:14-15; 21-25). Wash

with the Water of the Word. Seek the face of God. Make a
decision to resist temptation and remain pure. If you do miss
the mark, repent quickly and get back on track.

Your mind is a battlefield when you do not see yourself
the way God sees you. You feel like you have no power. You
talk yourself out of every move. In Judges six, an Angel
visited Gideon and referred to him as a "mighty man." Gideon
countered by sharing exactly how he saw himself, someone
from the weakest clan who was least in his family. He
mentally wrestled with that image before eventually receiving
and believing the words spoken over him. Those words gave
him courage (Judges 6).

Flesh will cause you to doubt yourself, misuse others, or
react by lashing out. You perpetually live in offense. No
matter how well meaning others are, everything they say
seems like a put down. God loves you and sees you as a
beautiful, powerful creature. He will perform great miracles
in your life. Draw near to Him in prayer, praise, and worship.
You can't do that if the devil has a stronghold in your mind.

Worship. Worship must be offered from a sanctified place. Old
Testament priests consecrated themselves and their place of
worship (Exodus 30:22 – 29) with anointing oil God instructed
Moses to make. Ingredients and portions were specified. It
was made with care and was to be reproduced by Priests only.
There were serious consequences for unsanctioned replication
(Exodus 30:31-33). The punishment was harsh. Even more
damaging was the fact this punishment would be meted out
after they began disconnecting themselves from God by
disobeying his command regarding the oil. Their existence
would become desolate.

God must be able to trust those who carry the anointing to
be authentic. There are precursors to becoming anointed to
serve. You must have a willing heart and a willing mind. There
must also be a strong desire to be true to God, your calling and
His people. The children of Israel failed at this in Exodus 33:1-
35. They were worshipping a golden calf.

Aaron, the priest, disqualified himself as one who could
carry the anointing. He was swayed by the people (into

creating this false God). He led them in worship, but did not take responsibility when Moses confronted him. The correct response should have been a penitent heart.

You cannot play with the anointing. If you do, not only will you suffer but those assigned to you will also. It was Moses who atoned for the people's sin, and they still endured a painful consequence (Exodus 32:35).

Position yourself to become an authentically anointed vessel. Draw the power of the Holy Spirit and produce a manifestation of miracles, signs and wonders. You will win souls for the Kingdom.

Worship must be offered from a place of purity. Your worship and gifts, hearing and choices, speech and thoughts, need to be consecrated and surrendered to God. It is easy to leave these areas open to the enemy. Being inaccurate in just one is certainly going to create havoc in the others. They are interconnected.

Wrong thoughts cause contaminated or distorted hearing, which affects speech and decisions and ultimately the way you choose to go through life. Purification prepares you for breakthrough. You must be sanctified if the anointing is going to rest on you. Let it draw the Holy Spirit. He will be a constant source of power.

Draw the Holy Spirit
The anointing invites the Holy Spirit to inhabit you. Samuel anointed David, with a "Horn of oil...in the presence of his brothers, and from that day on the Spirit of the LORD came upon David in power" (1 Samuel 16:13). That power sustained David in the field. It gave him supernatural strength. The anointing transformed his self-concept and his perspective. David did not put limitations on himself. He became a spiritual giant.

The anointing strengthens your relationship with God. There was no fear in David. He never considered an attack on a Philistine giant a suicide mission. He was not afraid of losing. A righteous anger stirred inside him when he heard Goliath's disrespectful stance against God and his people. He refused Saul's armor, knowing it would not protect him as well as the Spirit of God. It had no supernatural power. He knew the Holy Spirit was his most important weapon and it gave him courage. This strength, this power, this authority, is yours too.

On the day of Pentecost "a sound like the blowing of a violent wind came from heaven and filled the whole house where they were sitting ... All of them were filled with the Holy Spirit" (Acts 2:1-4). Jesus called it "the gift my Father promised" (Acts 1:4). The baptism of the Holy Spirit made the nature of Christ visible in the disciples and caused others to be drawn into the Kingdom (Luke 2:41). They added to their numbers daily (Luke 2:47).

Jesus prophesied the coming of the Holy Spirit (Acts 1:8), and that proclamation stirred the hearts of the disciples. When the Holy Spirit did come, they were bold and filled with a power that gave them courage to consistently deliver the message of the gospel of the Kingdom to those who were lost. That power creates real transformation, the kind that develops a God-centered heart attitude.

Transforms Your Heart
You are body, soul and spirit. More often than not, the body and soul rule until there is a revelation of Christ, and the spirit rises in stature and authority. Only then can you wrestle against principalities and powers. Jacob experienced this transformation. He was a cheat, a liar and a con artist. His soul dominated for most of his life, until he had a God encounter. God's love was his saving grace

There is an anointing for every purpose and calling. You cannot hijack an anointing, expecting to see good fruit. At best, you begin moving among God's people, speaking on His behalf without His blessing. What you reap has the potential to destroy you and corrupt the lives of others. It was not the birthright that Jacob bought from Esau that transformed his heart—it was the anointing he eventually received when God met him at Bethel (Genesis 32).

The anointing navigates you toward destiny. Through all of the deception and conniving behavior, Jacob was continually in a process of transformation. Everything he encountered brought him closer to a cataclysmic change which came when he wrestled with the Angel of God. In his wretchedness, he was being shaped to become father of a nation.

Before Jacob was born, his mother received a prophetic word from the Lord, declaring, "Two nations are in your womb, and two peoples from within you will be separated; one people will be stronger than the other, and the older will serve the younger" (Genesis 25:23). Jacob was the younger and Esau the older, but it was Jacob who was destined for greatness. Although he charted a course that was contrary to destiny, ultimately he came full circle; drawn back to the original purpose God had for his life.

The issue of the stolen birthright created a rift between Jacob and Esau, who was so angry he rejected Jacob for most of their lives. Eventually it was Jacob's fear of Esau that drove him to his knees. He orchestrated time alone for meditation and prayer in preparation to reconcile with Esau. God met Jacob then and completed a work that transformed his heart.

The anointing commands absolute obedience. Obedience yields a rise in stature in the eyes of God and man. Part of Jacob's requirement to fulfill purpose was reconnecting with Esau. Would God exponentially bless a contaminated life? No, and Jacob's purging began with a desire to restore his relationship with his brother.

The Bible says, "Whoever claims to love God yet hates a brother or sister is a liar. For whoever does not love their brother and sister, whom they have seen, cannot love God, whom they have not seen. And he has given us this command: Anyone who loves God must also love their brother and sister" (1 John 4:20). Jacob obeyed this command, and God intervened so that nothing he was promised would elude him.

Commands Obedience
Full obedience releases and increases the anointing. Abraham had special encounters with God. There was a powerful

blessing on his life, and an extraordinary anointing rested upon him. By the time he was asked to sacrifice his only son, there was no question about whether or not he would obey. He trusted God implicitly.

Instead of becoming anxious or afraid, he told the servants, "Stay here with the donkey while I and the boy go over there. We will worship and then we will come back to you" (Genesis 22:5). Fear did not cause Abraham to doubt or hide from God. He worshipped wholly, with heartfelt assurance that his son would be okay.

I sometimes imagine his journey to the place of sacrifice with a phrase playing over and over in his head, "Lord, I am going to do what You asked, and I know my son will be okay. I don't know how You are going to do it, but You will do it somehow."

Abraham's obedience secured Isaac's destiny. His purpose was established before birth, but was initiated during worship. It was through Isaac that Abraham's legacy continued. This should encourage you to trust God, even when you do not fully understand what He is doing in you. Eventually reasons become clear, often at the end of your process. Everything moves according to His ultimate plan when you trust and obey.

Initiates Purpose

Saul's purpose was activated when the anointing fell powerfully on his way to Damascus. He heard the voice of God and was miraculously transformed (Acts 9). He was a persecutor of Christians who was also called to be a Kingdom ambassador, proclaiming the name of Christ. His life changed, and he was no longer called Saul the persecutor, but Paul the Apostle. His life had greater purpose, but he also paid an enormous price.

No matter what he suffered, still he kept true to his calling. As he neared the end of life Paul encouraged those coming behind him to continue the work, testifying, "I have fought the good fight, I have finished the race, I have kept the faith. Now there is in store for me the crown of righteousness, which the Lord, the righteous Judge, will award to me on that day—and not only to me, but also to all who have longed for his appearing" (2 Timothy 4:7-8). Saul's spirit pushed him beyond natural determination to preach the Gospel at all costs. He remained a devout servant, apostle, and leader until he died, worshipping in spirit and in truth.

Cultivates Persistent Worship

The anointing cultivates persistent worship. Daniel's life was continual worship. Everything he did caused even unbelievers to begin to ponder the sovereignty of his God. Heathen kings bowed and commanded their Kingdoms to worship Him (Daniel 6). Daniel did not live one way before the king and another in private. His authenticity brought him great honor.

There is no worship if deception exists. Satan is the father of lies. He works in darkness. Darkness hides sin, and therefore the soul dies. Truth is light, and light illuminates the soul. It exposes anything not like God. In the light of the Word, repentance comes. It brings you to your knees, begging forgiveness and sanctification so that you may dwell in the Presence of God.

The persistent worshipper forges a path beyond challenges, frailties, and mistakes. They seek purity and long to be at the feet of God. David continually exposed his frailties and his transgressions. His desire was to remain pure (Psalm 119:33-40). Despite his mistakes, it was this characteristic which gave him a special place in God's heart. The blessing filtered down to his successor, Solomon, who was anointed to build God's holy place. That anointing prepared him for greatness.

Like David, persistent worshippers long for the presence of God. The relationship that develops secures their anointing. It also creates deeper humility in their hearts.

Prepares You to Rule

Jesus earned the right to rule over the Kingdoms of this world. He was an heir who could have stepped into the role without having to qualify. As Savior and Redeemer, His process of trials, testing and persecution serves as a sobering yet inspirational example. He was humble, obedient and respectful to His Father, and the earthly authority in whose charge He grew. Jesus felt pain and anger, compassion and love; yet was not driven by emotions. He loved others in spite of who they were and what they represented, yet never condoned sin. He Himself, knew no sin (2 Corinthians 5:21).

He was celebrated, rejected, afflicted and wounded, yet had courage to stand. He came through the womb to serve as the prototype for Kingdom ambassadors who impart the gospel. Because of His sacrifice you are free to rule and have dominion (Genesis 1:26). This cannot be done without righteousness. Adam and Eve's downfall demonstrated that clearly. Righteousness positions you to receive impartation of sustained power. That impartation equips you to carry the mantle.

IMPARTATION

Appoints You to Service

Jesus, knew His power, but was not driven by power. He was driven by purpose. This made it easy for Him to completely submit to the will of His Father. He was cloaked in humility, not insecurity. His desire was to fulfill righteousness, not build notoriety. He had a profound understanding of how to tap into Kingdom power, and was complete focused on the mission (Luke 4:18-21).

Many believe because they are called by God, the road should be easy, with solutions to every obstacle readily available. That is often furthest from the truth. Immediately after God bestowed the blessing of the Dove upon Jesus, He was "sent into the wilderness to be tempted by the devil" (Matthew 4:1). Even He was proved through hardship, shaped by adversity, and transformed in the fire.

Christ's submission caused an exponential explosion of the anointing to manifest in Him during the wilderness experience. There was nothing the devil could say to compel Him to sin. Instead the anointing caused the devil to leave Him and drew angels (Matthew 4:11).

After passing that test Jesus began preaching (Matthew 4:17). He had stepped out of the wilderness into purpose. He moved in faith, grace and power because He had been anointed and appointed by God.

The same can be true for you. Become a vessel fueled by

purpose. Be anointed for the Master's use. Move toward destiny determined to manifest God's glory so all may see and know Him.

Elisha was one who had that passion. It caused him to single mindedly pursue the anointing until he felt and saw its power. He carried Elijah's legacy until the day he died.

Secures the Legacy

An anointing simply obtained provides no opportunity for the giver to determine the commitment of the receiver. Elijah did not merely bestow an anointing upon Elisha. Elisha had to qualify to carry the legacy. Once qualified, he fully and accurately functioned in his assigned role.

The process started when he answered the call. His first thought was about the people he was leaving behind, not about the purpose that lay ahead (1Kings 19:20). He did not yet have unbroken focus.

Because of this, Elijah could not immediately embrace Elisha. He may have questioned himself, thinking, "I know I was instructed to select Elisha, Lord, but have I done it prematurely? Not only is his first thought about his parents; he left his earthly possessions (oxen/flesh) behind. He did not kill them." Elijah needed to know that Elisha understood exactly what the call meant. His entire life would be transformed. There could be nothing left behind that would create the temptation to abandon purpose.

In the process Elisha eventually understood, because he went back and, "took his yoke of oxen and slaughtered them ... burned the plowing equipment to cook the meat and gave it to the people" (1 Kings 19:21). He "set out to follow Elijah and became his servant" (1 Kings 19:21), focusing solely on following and serving. Elisha carried that lesson in his heart.

When Elijah told Elisha, "You have asked a difficult thing ... yet if you see me when I am taken from you, it will be yours—otherwise, it will not" (2 Kings 2:10), Elisha knew what he had to do. No matter where Elijah went, he followed. Each time people reminded him that Elijah's departure was imminent; he told them to be quiet. He did not want to focus on the fact that Elijah was leaving. He wanted to glean as much as he could with the time he had left. His mind had to be clear, his spirit ready to catch the anointing.

When Elijah was being taken up in the whirlwind, Elisha "Cried out, "My father! My father!" (2 Kings 2:12); and he kept looking for the mantle. That cloak was the conduit for the double portion anointing. Soon after he had it, Elisha began to move in faith. He placed his feet directly in Elijah's footprints by first parting the Jordan River like he had seen Elijah do (2 Kings 2:7-14).

There were others who could have received Elijah's mantle, if they had done what was necessary to qualify. They would not sacrifice personal plans to carry the inheritance. They had not reduced themselves so that God could be built up in them. They were not fashioned as legacy bearers. Because Elisha paid the price, when he received the anointing, its power was acknowledged (2 Kings 2:13-15).

A strong foundation secures the legacy. Premature babies sometimes die. When they do not, they often have to fight to live. Some deal with physical abnormalities and other ailments because they were not in the womb long enough to come to full maturation. Those who survive receive extensive care and nurturing until they are able to thrive on their own. This is also true spiritually. You cannot rush into ministry before you are fully mature without risking injury.

Full spiritual gestation must be achieved to establish a strong foundation that will withstand anything and be capable of handling God designed assignments. Jesus [speaking to His disciples] said, "Anyone who wants to be first must be the very last, and the servant of all" (Mark 9:35). Many times those rushing to be first are the most immature. Elisha did not immediately begin functioning in the office of a prophet. He was Elijah's servant first. As he served, he grew and developed greater focus and understanding of his assignments.

An honorable spirit births the desire to please God and present a noble tribute. By the time Elijah's departure from earth was near, Elisha had locked in on the principles, functions, focus and weight of his call. He knew that to continue serving well, it was necessary to carry an anointing

greater than Elijah's. Elisha asked for a double portion because
he earned the right to an inheritance from his spiritual father.
He had become a son (2 Kings 2:9).

No process, no anointing. You cannot be afraid to willingly
sacrifice the flesh and remain humble. Don't see yourself as
greater than you are and miss principles that secure a strong
foundation (knowledge and grace) required to carry the mantle.
You must honorably present the legacy of Jesus Christ. How
can you do that if you are incapable of walking as He walked,
loving as He loved, serving as He served and living in humility
and purpose?

   You position yourself for the anointing when you embrace
and cloak your spirit in Christ-likeness. The mantle can be
yours – but you must qualify. There is no possibility of
successful qualification if your spirit is not right. You need to
be aligned with the Word of God before you can obtain the
anointing. It prepares you for the weight of the call, because
sons and daughters receive the legacy but are not exempt from
the responsibility that is part of their inheritance.

RESPONSIBILITY

Can Christ Be Seen In You?
Do you reflect Christ in all you say and do? Are your thoughts
and actions in line with His Word? Does your life draw others
to Him? Are they interested in learning more about who He is
because of your walk? *Can Christ be seen in you?*

   The anointing rested on the Apostles because they were
willing vessels who had experienced and benefited from the
process (the call, purification, redemption, identification of
purpose, and a resolve to carry the Gospel of the Kingdom
throughout all the earth). They were not perfect; they had to be
proven. Christ sought them, prepared them, prayed for them,
and sent the Holy Spirit to do the rest (Acts 2:1-4). He
validated their imperfections as effective tools to draw others
with whom they could empathize. Just like their stories
affected many around them, your story will impact others too.

One account that stirred my heart was a presentation of Stephen's life in Acts six. The Bible refers to him as "A man full of God's grace and power" (Acts 6:8). It says that, "He performed great wonders and signs among the people" (Acts 6:8); and as he did this, "Opposition arose ... from members of the Synagogue of the Freedmen (as it was called)—Jews of Cyrene and Alexandria as well as the provinces of Cilicia and Asia—who began to argue with Stephen. But they could not stand up against the wisdom the Spirit gave him as he spoke" (Acts 6:9-10). Since they could not stand against the words uttered because of the anointing he carried, they plotted to falsely accuse him of blasphemy (Acts 6:11-14).

In the face of accusations, Stephen could not be shaken (Acts 6:15). The examples he looked to were people like Abraham, Joseph, and Moses; individuals who were anointed to withstand persecution for the sake of the Kingdom (Acts 7:1-58). Their stance displayed a resolve that Stephen embraced. Their stories compelled him to stand in the face of danger. He spoke boldly and passionately, saying "I see heaven open and the Son of Man standing at the right hand of God" (Acts 7:56). There was no fear in him. The testimony of those who had gone before gave him courage.

Stephen's death highlighted a valiant display of the life of a Kingdom Warrior. He prayed for those who hurt him (Acts 7:59-60). Just as Jesus said, "Father, forgive them for they know not what they do" (Luke 23:34, NLT), Stephen extended that same grace and this had a powerful impact.

There was a young man named Saul (Acts 7:58) at Stephen's execution, who had zealously persecuted Christians. His heart began changing as he watched the display of Stephen's staunch faith and he was transformed in a way he never imagined. It was the beginning of Saul's move toward purpose.

Your Anointing Can Save Others
There was something about Stephen's assassination that made it impossible for Saul to shake those last moments from his mind. It softened his heart and made it pliable to God's dealings. Earlier in this chapter, you read about the fact that

he was on his way to persecute Christians (Acts 9:3-12) when he had an encounter with Jesus. That set the atmosphere for a powerful experience which revolutionized his life.

When I first met my husband, Bruce, and began developing a friendship with him, I was in a backslidden state. I visited church on Sunday mornings, hoping to find something to anchor me. I tried to kill the constant nagging that something in my life was out of place. God had been tugging on my heart and I was trying to listen, but did what I wanted to do at the same time. When I finally answered Him, we had already begun dating. God's call was strong, the anointing concentrated. I immediately told Bruce there was no way I could continue to see him, explaining that I had made a decision to follow Jesus, and nothing could come before that commitment.

The transformation God had done in my heart was complete. No matter how much I'd begun to love and care for Bruce, I had no desire to remain in a relationship with him if it displeased God. It hurt my heart, and I know it hurt his, but for me there was no other way.

Fast forward more than six months. He began inviting me to bible study. As far as I knew, he was not a Christian (not even interested in the Word) and I believed this invitation was a smoke screen; a way to get me out on a date and draw me back into a relationship. I was focused on God, and I did not want to be distracted.

Several months later he said, "Everyone can see the change in my life but you." I wanted there to be a change, but I wanted him to desire a relationship with God for himself, not because he wanted to be with me.

By that time, I had become a part of the worship team and began volunteering in the church office. One Sunday morning, in the middle of our service, I noticed a man in one of the rear pews of the church enthralled in worship, his face aglow. It was Bruce, and I knew that God had found him. I wanted to know how his life was transformed. After our wedding, he shared a testimony that blew my mind.

Basically when I put God first, Bruce began trying to find out about this God. Who was He that someone who loved him would walk away without reservation and be unrelenting in their resolve? Who was this God that was so worthy, so deserving of a passionate love which transcended the natural? He started searching, found a bible study group, and began to learn about God for himself.

I could not help but think, what if I hadn't said yes to God? What if I had not been sold out to Him completely? What if I made a decision to answer the call to purpose and then relented at Bruce's persistent expression of love? What if I had not decided to honor God with my life? My husband's life may have been very different, and mine too. Thank God for the anointing that initiates the call and establishes purpose (Acts 2:22-28).

I could not save Bruce, but my resolve to stand as a believer awakened a desire in his heart to allow God to draw him close. Please understand how much your life can become a testimony. It has the ability to encourage others toward a path to transformation. Protect your anointing. Walk in the way of the Lord and live a lifestyle of worship.

Protect the Anointing

In Genesis chapters thirty-seven to fifty, Joseph's life is chronicled. It is understood early in the narrative that there was a strong anointing on him to rule. His process toward governance was strewn with one encounter after another which challenged his purity and threatened to derail progress. Thankfully, his experiences were only able to delay him, because time after time, Joseph chose to do what was right.

His brothers threw him into a pit (Genesis 37:23-24). He was sold into slavery, more than once (Genesis 37:28-29, 36). Although he ended up as Potiphar's slave, his anointing grew because he knew how to protect it (Genesis 39:3-4). Joseph did all tasks with great excellence. His anointing drew added favor on his life and on his master's house (Genesis 39:5). It also expanded his assignment (Genesis 39:6). In the midst of this favor, Potiphar's wife tried to entice Joseph to commit adultery (Genesis 39:7). He was faced with a challenge. She was relentless in her pursuit. He had to repeatedly choose between dishonoring God and remaining a loyal son (Genesis 39:10).

It is not always easy to protect the anointing. There is a great price to pay for staying true to your conviction. Joseph did not consider the price he would pay for standing. While saying yes may have held his position in the household, saying no was the right thing to do. This choice landed him in jail. He was an innocent man, incarcerated for doing what was right, yet he protected his anointing and glorified God with his decisions.

Limitations do not hamper the anointing, they increase it. In prison, Joseph found favor with the warden, and was put in charge of the entire facility. He had keys to the place of his confinement and could have used them to leave at any time; but he did not. Instead, the anointing on his life drew the instrument (the cupbearer) God would use to elevate Joseph in the prison. That person had been a worker in the palace, yet found himself in a jail cell with Joseph (Genesis 40:1-4).

God gave Joseph opportunities to display his gift and anointing to Pharaoh's baker and his cupbearer, yet only one carried the seed of deliverance that would fully propel him into his role as a leader. It was the cupbearer (a man the king trusted with his life) who told the king about Joseph and he summoned him to the palace.

To handle the weight of the assignment, the anointing must flow powerfully and continually. Joseph protected the anointing. His reward was great, but so was the responsibility. God caused Pharaoh to "Put [him] in charge of the whole land of Egypt. Then Pharaoh took his signet ring from his finger and put it on Joseph's finger. He dressed him in robes of fine linen and put a gold chain around his neck. He had him ride in a chariot as his second-in-command, and people shouted before him, "Make way!" Thus he put him in charge of the whole land of Egypt (Genesis 41:41-43).

A perpetual stand for what was right had drawn exponential promotion. Joseph never compromised himself. He never compromised the anointing.

Walk Uprightly before God

There was no question that Joseph honored God. His heart was focused on the promise and the provision on his life. He was not lax in the responsibility to do everything he could to reach destiny. His decisions caused others to see the nature of His God. It also brought favor and grace to endure the process of preparation. God needed him to stand so His glory and character would be revealed to many (Genesis 42 – 47).

Joseph also forgave his brothers and brought rest to the heart of a father who had still been grieving for him. The nation of Israel was saved by his actions.

You are a gem in the Kingdom of God. You are precious in His eyes, but not infallible. You try, you fail; you get up and start again. The key is to become completely sold out until there is no question that, no matter what comes, you will press beyond yourself to honor and accurately represent the heavenly Father. Hold on to your conviction.

Jesus said, "Very truly I tell you, the Son can do nothing by himself; he can do only what he sees his Father doing, because whatever the Father does the Son also does" (John 5:19). This is all you need to walk uprightly before God.

Another example is Daniel. He was obedient, humble, and his worship, drew the power of the anointing. It saved him from the Lions and secured his future. After he was delivered from the lions, a pagan King acknowledged his God before a heathen nation, saying, "I issue a decree that in every part of my kingdom people must fear and reverence the God of Daniel. For he is the living God and he endures forever; his kingdom will not be destroyed, his dominion will never end" (Daniel 6:26).

Your pure walk will let others see God's nature in you. Daniel's devotion and steadfastness brought assurance to the king's heart. He trusted Daniel's God and wanted his people to share that trust. When you walk uprightly before God, Kingdom expansion is inevitable.

Expand the Kingdom

The Apostles in Acts two presented a pure, unadulterated

witness of Kingdom to the world. You can too, through your life and ministry. Do not be fearful about presenting Christ everywhere you go. Go where you have been called. Everyone will not accept you, but you must speak the Word regardless.

The Apostles preached, "Therefore let all Israel be assured of this: God has made this Jesus, whom you crucified, both Lord and Messiah…Repent and be baptized, every one of you, in the name of Jesus Christ for the forgiveness of your sins. And you will receive the gift of the Holy Spirit"(Acts 2:36, 38). It was not a popular message. There were many detractors, yet three thousand souls were added at one time! If the people of God collectively do this, the number of new souls in the Kingdom would be limitless.

The Bible says, "Seek first the Kingdom of God, and His righteousness" (Matthew 6:33), but that means different things to different people because many lack understanding. For others to be influenced by your God centered lifestyle, they must hear and also understand the message being shared (Matthew 13:23). If your hearing or your spirit is blocked, you will push people away from Christ.

Jesus commissioned the disciples, saying, "Go and make disciples of all nations, baptizing them in the name of the Father and of the Son and of the Holy Spirit, and teaching them to obey everything I have commanded you" (Matthew 28:19-20). He also told them that "The gospel of the Kingdom shall be preached in all the world for a witness to all nations" (Matthew 24:14).

How will the gospel of the Kingdom be preached in the entire world? Who are the witnesses? If not you, then who? Your life must speak more loudly than your words.

Contaminated spirits will not bring souls into the Kingdom.
Elisha's servant (Gehazi) lost position and the ability to fulfill purpose because of his infected spirit. He gained things by lying to Naaman, and lying on Elisha. He compounded the situation by hiding his sin. The contamination in Gehazi's heart eventually became visible on his flesh (leprosy). His affliction would contaminate others. He was no longer fit to serve (2 Kings 5:25-27).

A pure walk convicts hearts. Naaman's life changed after his healing. He was willing to take a stand in the midst of a pagan society. His spirit would no longer allow him to continue serving a false God. He was touched, physically and spiritually, by the miracle and became even more convinced of the authenticity of Elisha's anointing. He saw the nature of Elisha's God and vowed to acknowledge and worship Him only (2 Kings 5:15-18).

You can make the same impact in your society and other regions of the world. You are called to accurately present the God you serve through a lifestyle of worship and devotion; nothing less. If you do this, there will be powerful transformation. You will impact lives to enlarge the Kingdom. "Hold fast the profession of your faith without wavering" (Hebrews 10:23, KJV) as God divinely uses you to build Zion.

Although Elisha set a great example, Gehazi never became a son. His choices were contrary to the principles displayed by Elisha. He served, but was never truly plugged in. It is a dangerous thing. This disconnection becomes a doorway for spiritual infections to insidiously block the anointing and derail purpose. Be careful not to obstruct the power of the oil in your life. God wants to use you, but you must chart the right course.

╬

Prayer

Lord, make me a vessel fit for your use, completely devoted, transformed by your grace. May others see you enthroned in my heart; long for the same – desire to be part, of your Kingdom.

Help me to walk right, live right, do right. Give me the will to consistently choose right; Understanding Lord that the life of my brother, the life of my sister, may just depend on a choice that I've made; a part that I've played. Lord, make me a worthy vessel.
In Jesus' Name - Amen

Chapter Three

✑
THE POWER OF THE OIL

When tires on a car are not properly aligned, the vehicle may go off course. The wheels wear faster and eventually become unusable. They take the car and the occupants where they need to go, but it is not safe. The results could be disastrous. To a seasoned driver, the forward movement of a grossly misaligned car feels treacherous, but to a novice all is normal. They are ignorantly unaware of the danger that could ultimately lead to their demise or cause harm to others.

You must be able to discern truth from error so your anointing is not hindered. An individual with no *covenant* can operate in an anointing, but will have no authority. Someone who haphazardly functions despite intermittent communication with the Father (*no prayer life*), who observes lying vanities (*no discernment*), who is unkind toward others (*no love*) or spends no time in the Word (*no growth, no life*), can only offer a contaminated word. They are like that car with severely misaligned wheels, carrying passengers who may be unaware of the dangers. Their lives will reflect deficits.

Conversely, someone who has been called, who consistently stays connected to God, is properly positioned to operate in the power of the anointing. They correctly relate to the ones to whom they are assigned. Word of knowledge, prophesy and the gift of discernment will operate fully, and grow to new dimensions through grace and constant function.

The Oil Magnifies Your Anointing

When you are properly positioned and prepared, you become a powerfully effective instrument; armed with precision. Samuel was called and anointed at a very young age. The level of the oil singled him out as a true messenger. His ears and his heart were open. He lived with the Ark (Presence) and was in place for a greater anointing (1 Samuel 3:8-11). This happened during a time when God rarely spoke to or gave visions to others (1 Samuel 3:1-4).

Proper positioning increases discernment. When the prophet Ezekiel "was among the exiles by the Kebar River, the heavens were opened and [he] saw visions of God" (Ezekiel 1:1). Near the end of the vision, he "fell facedown, and [he] heard the voice of one speaking" (Ezekiel 1:28). The voice said, "Son of man, stand up on your feet and I will speak to you"(Ezekiel 2:1). Ezekiel's posture strengthened the anointing. He was properly positioned to see. He was worshipful, reverent, and endowed by the Spirit to move. His visions and instructions were specific and powerful, all because of the anointing.

A strengthened anointing breaks yokes. The children of Israel were in bondage in Egypt. Freedom seemed an unattainable dream. God sent Moses to demand their freedom, yet he felt himself incapable of handling the assignment. He was anointed for the task (Exodus 3:10), and the anointing broke through Pharaoh's resistance until the Israelites were free. The same was true for Gideon.

In his case, the Midianites were oppressing the children of Israel. Gideon was sure there was no way he could lead an army that would defeat his enemies, but God anointed him for the task. He called him, "Mighty Warrior" (Judges 6:12). He did not feel like a warrior, but the anointing empowered him (Judges 6:14). If you read the rest of this chapter, you will see that Gideon was never alone. He was directed and reassured until he had victory.

Do not go where you have not been sent. Don't try to move in your own strength. Wait for the command and the anointing of the Lord and watch what God does through you. If either

Moses or Gideon had attempted to fulfill purpose without God, they would have failed. It was the call and the anointing that gave them supernatural ability to accomplish what they were sure was impossible.

Protects your Gift & Purpose

The anointing is a precious gift. It covers servants of God who are living on purpose. It will not manifest if your life is not drawing it toward you. Intimacy with God protects the anointing. Without the oil, you are powerless against the wiles of the devil, and will not be able to bring about lasting transformation.

Prophetic words may manifest in lives of people who are unprepared, ill equipped or inaccurately assigned because your revelation did not come from the throne of God. They eventually destroy the individual. You have a responsibility to remain plugged into the source of true revelation and speak only what He says. If you don't, the enemy will use you for target practice.

The anointing protects the gift. A great example of this truth was seen when the Apostle Paul was bitten by a poisonous snake on the island of Malta. The Holy Spirit shielded him by ensuring that the poisonous venom did no harm to his body (Acts 28:3-5). Paul's faith, and protection from the anointing, safeguarded him. It allowed him to continue preaching the gospel of the Kingdom wherever he was sent. This anointed dimension deflects the enemy's attacks.

The anointing is lost when wrong choices are made deliberately. The heart of the mission and the messenger are exposed to shrewd tactics and volatile attacks from the enemy. Sampson lost his anointing and experienced spiritual decapitation when he allowed his heart to become contaminated by Delilah. His purpose could not be fulfilled in that state. He became weak, helpless, hopeless, and desolate – because the Spirit of the Lord left him (Judges 16:15-21).

It was only after Samson was in prison that he began to commune with God once again. This strengthened and realigned him. Suddenly there was a reestablished connection. When the anointing returned so did Samson's strength (Judges 16:22, 28). God heard his prayer, and that day, he killed more than three thousand, including all the rulers of Philistine (Judges 16:27-30). His final act of repentance caused the anointed gift to accomplish its goal.

Wrong association is catastrophic to the anointing. Who are you hanging with? What are they saying to you? What are you saying to them? What do you do together? Does it help or hurt individual or corporate destiny? These are key questions that must be asked and answered. I have made the mistake of fostering connections that were detrimental. If not for that still small voice urging me to be careful or instructing me to retreat, it would have been *more* disastrous.

Continually ask the Holy Spirit for discernment. Know the spirit of individuals with whom you connect. Samson's life was altered because of wrong attachment. Strive to maintain the anointing that breaks the yoke. Do not invite and tolerate yokes that break the anointing.

Destroys the Yoke

The assignment you are anointed for has requirements. It will ask hard things of you. When you are obedient to the Lord it is going to antagonize some people. Even those you think are most likely to understand may disappoint you by reacting in ways that create a break in the relationship. Many times that break happens because your connection to them has distracted you from fulfilling purpose. It is only after it shatters that you come to yourself. Your heart is tender, malleable, desiring closer contact with God. You long to feel His comfort, hear His voice and receive fresh revelation to equip you for the next phase of your purpose.

Do not spend time pining for the connection, instead use the time to plug into God and dig deep for greater dimensions of Him. When you get to a state of complete reliance upon the Holy Spirit, the anointing assigned to the yoke is activated and released.

The yoke may not be removed, but its power to reduce and

defeat you is immediately cancelled. It can no longer bind you and hinder the work you have been called to accomplish. The anointing destroys it (Isaiah 10:27). Thank God for the anointing. It annihilates the power of all bondage and provides supernatural ability to manifest the Kingdom.

Your cross does not feel burdensome if you function under the anointing. Purpose manifests, and it propels you into destiny. Jesus said, "Take my yoke upon you and learn from me, for I am gentle and humble in heart, and you will find rest for your souls. For my yoke is easy and my burden is light" (Matthew 11:29-30). Right after He made this declaration, He went around displaying great miracles of healing. It was an active demonstration designed by God to verify that Jesus had spoken truth.

You cannot be used to heal if your soul is so torn up, broken down or contaminated that it repels the anointing. No anointing equals no power. Jesus' purity, gentleness, humility and peace allowed His anointing to be potent.

Manifests Healing

In this section, I will focus on healing of the soul. There are some requirements that must be met to keep the flow of anointed power circulating. The first step is to repent and ask and receive forgiveness of your sins (2 Timothy 2:19). This is where true healing begins. After repentance, comes the actual work of becoming a "vessel unto honour, sanctified, and meet for the master's use, and prepared unto every good work" (2 Timothy 2:21). Get into the Word of God. Allow it to change your mind and heart and you will grow in grace and knowledge.

Become a member of an active and accurate local church. As you grow, you need a spiritual father and mother to be accountable to, and brothers and sisters whose fellowship can help you to stand, even in times when you are most challenged. Be built up and equipped for Kingdom work. Timothy also provides other practical steps toward progress and full healing.

Flee also youthful lusts: but follow righteousness, faith, charity, peace, with them that call on the Lord out of a pure heart. But foolish and unlearned questions avoid, knowing that they do gender strifes. Be gentle unto all men, apt to teach, patient, in meekness instructing those that oppose themselves; if God peradventure will give them repentance to the acknowledging of the truth (2 Timothy 2:22-25).

Jesus will heal your soul and make you whole. He will repair emotional fractures, revolutionize your thought patterns and allow you to use your story for someone else's deliverance. The freedom of healing ignites a fire in your heart. Before long, you can feel the anointing flowing over you, into you, and through you. Do not take it lightly, treasure it. Guard it from contamination and hangers-on who wish to share in the fruit of the labor, but will never come alongside you in the process of preparation. Maintain a lifestyle that keeps the anointing flowing to place you on a path where you "prosper, even as your soul prospers" (3 John 1:2).

Draws Prosperity

To draw prosperity, humility and total surrender must be an integral part of your DNA. David asked God to "wash him thoroughly from iniquity and cleanse him from sin" (Psalm 51:2). He wanted a clean heart and a right spirit. He asked to remain in the presence of God, to maintain a constant connection to the Holy Spirit (Psalm 51:10-12). He was preparing himself for a continual flow of the anointing.

Throughout the Psalms, David speaks of his unending desire for more of God. He repented often and worked diligently to right his wrongs. He remained plugged into the Spirit. As a result, the anointing rested on him and prosperity followed. He was not a perfect man; he made many mistakes, but it was the attitude of David's heart that caused the oil to flow. In Psalm 23, he says,

The Lord is my shepherd; I shall not want. He makes me lie down in green pastures. He leads me beside still waters. He restores my soul. He leads me in paths of righteousness for his name's sake.

Even though I walk through the valley of the shadow of
death, I will fear no evil, for you are with me; your rod and
your staff, they comfort me. You prepare a table before me
in the presence of my enemies; you anoint my head with
oil; my cup overflows (vs. 1-6).

The oil is the last thing mentioned in these verses, but the
precursors are clear. David surrendered to *and* allowed himself
to be led by the Lord. He experienced peace, and restoration.
He had no fear, because his faith and confidence were in the
God he served. He was willing and committed. It was after
David began living in this state that the anointing poured over
him. His cup was filled to overflowing.

**Many want the anointing but don't want to meet simple
requirements**. How can a leaking vessel contain the oil?
Contamination causes it to seep out and flow into places
unworthy of its presence. It becomes wasted; settling in
containers that cannot hold it. It becomes diluted with other
substances. For example, it was wasted on the sons of the
priest, Eli. They defiled themselves and the Temple of the Most
High God. It was just not in them to live a life of honor (1
Samuel 2:12).

Contamination will cut you off from the Lord. The pure Word
cannot dwell in the bosom of a soul that harbors venomous
contaminants. Purity is necessary to receive accurate
revelation from God. Without it, every word received and
imparted is contaminated. Do not kill the anointing because of
dreadful choices that bring dishonor.
God could not speak to Eli's sons because they would not
hear Him. He had to move them out of the way. The anointing
could not rest upon them. Their persistent disrespect cost them
their lives (1 Samuel 2:34).

Brings Revelation
When the anointing is present, revelation comes unhindered.
John spoke of the anointing that brings revelation, saying, "But

the anointing that you received from him abides in you, and
you have no need that anyone should teach you. But as his
anointing teaches you about everything, and is true, and is no
lie—just as it has taught you, abide in him" (1 John 2:27). He
explained that you must be positioned to receive the proceeding
(Rhema) Word from God.

God anoints those He can trust to advance the Kingdom.
The anointing causes your spirit to not only be connected
directly to God, but to also be open to words of knowledge,
prophetic utterances, visions, dreams, and revelations. He
spoke to Daniel, Joseph and Jesus. They had knowledge of
things to come.

He elevated them to great dimensions of favor and
undergirded them in intense periods of suffering. Great grace is
required to bear up under the weight of both the call and the
message. The power of the anointing was enough to carry them
through the best and the worst of times.

Ushers Grace

Grace is possible because of the anointing. They are partners
that work together to complete God sized assignments. The
anointing without grace is like trying to go online without the
internet. The computer is turned on, but without an internet
connection, there is no access to browse. Jesus Christ had
supernatural grace to endure the cross and speak as His
Father spoke without fear of consequence.

Grace gave Daniel, a Kingdom son planted in captivity, the
fortitude to manage persecution. Joseph carried grace as well.
He suffered, endured and overcame. Their stories are deeply
embedded in biblical historical accounts which chronicle
journeys in both adverse and triumphant circumstances.

Paul's anointing drew grace and he carried it in his heart.
A great measure was extended to him because of the work he
was called to accomplish. Paul spoke of it to the people of
Ephesus, "Surely you have heard about the administration of
God's grace that was given to me for you, that is, the mystery
made known to me by revelation"(Ephesians 3:2-3). While the
call may initiate the anointing, to carry it, grace must abound.

When the anointed receive the covering and protection of grace, God encounters follow.

Ensures God Encounters

Jacob experienced amazing God encounters. He started out as a conniving thief, but once he stopped running and his heart came to a place of repentance; the anointing and grace were activated. They created the right environment in his heart. Jacob was on his way to make amends with his brother, Esau when he met the angel of the Lord (Genesis 32:1). He was afraid of Esau's wrath, yet persisted in seeking him out to repair the relationship. Do not count yourself out. You may have veered off course, but if you get your heart right; God will re-initiate and reactivate your anointing.

God restored Jacob and He will restore you. Restoration gave Jacob an even greater spiritual encounter. He wrestled with God for *the* blessing, and for full reinstatement to Kingdom purpose. When he was battle worn and broken, God validated him, saying, "Your name will no longer be Jacob, but Israel, because you have struggled with God and with humans and have overcome" (Genesis 32:28). Jacob's mind and spirit were changed. He stepped into the sweet, fragrant oil of the anointing which had been bestowed upon him at birth.

You must spend time alone with God to move beyond your struggle. Sometimes, the crowd will "crowd" His voice right out of your life if you let them. Make time to be in His Presence—to speak and to listen. Only ears that are attuned to the Spirit hear the call and accurately understand their assignment. Drown out the noise with worship and praise. Still the distraction of unwanted activity and become saturated by the Holy Spirit's fragrance. He speaks in whispers in this atmosphere. He imparts the anointing that equips you for service.

Calls You to the Royal Priesthood and Develops Kingdom Stature

John the Baptist was called before birth, yet had to achieve a stature in the spirit in order to fulfill God's call on His life. As a Saint, you are "Kings and priests unto God" (Revelations 1:6,

KJV). This call is initiated when you repent and Christ's blood washes and cleanses you. Your standing does not rise unless you grow in grace.

Plugging into God moves you toward destiny. He builds a strong foundation that anchors you. He establishes a kingdom culture in your spirit, a culture which becomes a springboard for everything He has purposed. Christ the man allowed himself to be developed, and built up to a place of stature in the spirit. He called people to serve, drove out evil spirits, and healed the sick and downcast.

First Peter chapter two verses four to five says, "As you come to him, the living Stone—rejected by humans but chosen by God and precious to him—you also, like living stones, are being built into a spiritual house to be a holy priesthood, offering spiritual sacrifices acceptable to God through Jesus Christ." You are prepared in obscurity and revealed at the time of God's choosing.

John's ministry was in the wilderness. He spent a lot of time alone with the Lord and lived a life of extreme sacrifice. God revealed things to him that he could not reveal to others. John experienced spiritual development that strengthened and enfolded him with uncommon boldness.

He preached of Jesus. He baptized in the name of Jesus and spoke out fiercely against hypocrites (Matthew 2-3). He willingly went into obscurity and embraced the process.

The season of preparation exposes, so much of what you go through during this time needs to be kept private until God releases you to share your testimony with others. Do not look for sympathy and coddling in your wilderness. Those simply sympathizing with you help to extend the journey of scourging or shaking designed to tear you down and build you up again. It is not compassion that you need, but people who have an understanding of the spiritual process. You need people who will pray for God's perfect will to be done in your life as you wait. Remember when Job was severely tested? God did not seek to comfort him, instead "The LORD spoke to Job out of the storm: 'Brace yourself like a man; I will question you, and you shall answer me. Would you discredit my justice? Would you condemn me to justify yourself?" (Job 7:6-10).

Not only did God not comfort him, he challenged Job, in essence saying, "You are going through a rough time right now, but you must remember I am the same God who prospered you before. Did you forget? Instead of reflecting on that, you seek to question my judgment about not quickly restoring your standing in the eyes of your friends and society. Well guess what, it is more important to maintain stature. Get ready for the questions I will ask, because they are coming fast and hard" [Paraphrased Job 7:6-10). God gave Job what he needed, not what he wanted.

Do not run from your wilderness experience. It is part of your making. Immediately after John baptized Jesus, He was led by the Spirit to the wilderness (Matthew 4:1). That experience exposed His stature. He spoke the Word with authority and power. He defeated the devil with the force of His light. He could have called the Host of Heaven to annihilate the enemy, but He simply reverted to what sustained Him—the Word (Matthew 4:1).

Do not allow pressure to distract you from your assignment. Let's be real. Laying flesh on the altar over and over again is hard. You have to make a decision to submit to God's way and follow through. Read the Book of Jeremiah. He was ostracized, persecuted, and imprisoned. At one time or another, he wanted to walk away from what God called him to do. It sometimes seemed too much to handle, but the oil of the anointing was ignited by the Holy Spirit. It motivated him to do as God asked. He was driven by an innate desire to please the Lord.

The wilderness will drive you to your knees. Your attitude in the place of trial matters greatly. It will make you long for God, humble your spirit, cause you to find a place in worship and release the power. It determines how you will go through. Immediately after Christ resisted the devil's temptation in the wilderness, He began displaying the power with which He had been endowed. Forty days and nights of testing did not decrease His authority, rather it became magnified.

The Children of Israel had a different experience. They grumbled, complained, and longed to go back to the place of bondage (Egypt) because it seemed easier to handle. They were focused on circumstances, desiring to escape the challenges that not only brought freedom, but would eventually lead them into a promised place of prosperity (Exodus 16). If they had patiently gone through the process, the experience would have been much different.

Oil garnered in the wilderness comes at great cost. There is plenty of oil in the wilderness but you must press beyond the flesh to draw it to you. In your most broken state, when your focus is solely on God; He can share secrets that you would not hear otherwise. He will direct you into areas you could not navigate on your own. During those times God determines how much He can trust you. How are you handling your process? Are you angry? Bitter? Impatient? Is your spirit humbly receiving from Him? Your disposition will either hurt or help. If you allow the flesh to dominate in the wilderness, you will prolong the process.

Be careful not to use the anointing for fleshly purposes. It is important to know what God has anointed you to do. Remember in Chapter One we talked about King David's son, Adonijah, who tried to hijack the throne? He thought he could assume a function and position that was not his to claim, and was able to convince key people in the kingdom to follow him. Why? Because something on the inside of them responded to what was in him. When it became clear that he would fail, Adonijah ran to the Temple, to the horns of the altar—not to repent, not to worship; but to try to preserve his flesh/life (1 Kings 1-53).

A convergence of similar anointings either helps or hurts Kingdom purpose. Individuals with like anointings draw each other through a subconscious attraction or connection. No good can come of joined anointings that are perverted. This was the case with Adonijah who "exalted himself saying, I will be king" (1 Kings 1:5, KJV). He was joined by "Joab and Abiathar the priest: and they following Adonijah helped him" (1 Kings 1:7, KJV). They were not attempting to manifest God's will for the nation of Israel. The focus was singular: exploit the physical weakness of King David to gain control of the Kingdom (1 Kings 1:1-53). This is a principle of Lucifer, fueled by a renegade spirit, a contaminated vessel.

Lucifer said, "I will ascend into heaven, I will exalt my throne above the stars of God: I will sit also upon the mount of the congregation, in the sides of the north: I will ascend above the heights of the clouds; I will be like the most High" (Isaiah 14:13-14). He had an elevated sense of self, and look where it got him. One third of the heavenly host followed him into a kingdom of darkness. Adonijah, Joab and Abiathar operated in these principles, to their ruin.

The devil empowers those he converts. If you allow him to, he will pervert your purpose. Joab was anointed to lead as a warrior in the court of King David, but he had a *renegade* spirit. He used his office to retaliate against Abner, although King David was at peace with Abner. Joab killed him in secret, knowing the King would not be pleased (2 Samuel 3:22-38). When he committed this treacherous act, he unleashed a spirit of vengeance and murder over Israel. Almost immediately Rekab and Baanah went into King Ishbosheth's house and killed him (2 Samuel 4:5-12). Converged demonic anointings cause undue harm.

Renegade anointings are driven by arrogance, and a blatant disregard for spiritual protocols. Pride is the precursor. Once that is allowed in, it is difficult to see any error in thought or deed. Their infiltration into Kingdom processes is serpentine in nature – sinuous – insidious – unwanted, slithering in and hiding in the dark until the enemy is ready to strike. Abiathar had been loyal to David (1 Samuel 22:20), but somewhere in his journey, he allowed contamination to enter his spirit. If this were not so, it would have been easy for him to refuse when Adonijah sought his help in commandeering the throne. They tried to hijack authority.

Pride grossly distorts perspective and focus. Lucifer saw himself in a position that could never be his, a position he was neither worthy nor capable of assuming. He sought a role that was only God's. He was blinded to inadequacies and thought himself infallible. Pride magnified the nonexistent exalted place where he imagined he should be positioned.

United spiritual power will cause miraculous manifestations of God's influence in any situation, and transform the lives of all involved in the process. In Acts sixteen, when Paul and Silas were beaten and imprisoned, they made a decision to praise God anyway. They maintained an attitude of power and authority, even in the degradation of the prison. Anointings joined in prayer, praise and worship (Acts 16:25). They were men of stature who maintained their standing in the midst of tribulation.

When those anointings converged, power reverberated beyond the area of confinement. "There was such a violent earthquake that the foundations of the prison were shaken. At once all the prison doors flew open, and everyone's chains came loose" (Acts 16:26). Nothing could stop the force of the power their anointings generated. Synergized unity drew a strong, swift response from Heaven.

The stature required to represent God does not happen overnight. Consider Samuel who was required to leave his parents as a very young boy, to be positioned in the Temple with Eli to be trained. He was called before he was born, but was not ready to step into that calling. It did not automatically guarantee kingdom stature. He was taken out of a familiar environment and thrust into the unfamiliar to be shaped and molded. The discomfort this shift brought caused him to press into God more. He needed nurturing, sustenance, assurance, comfort, strength and direction. In the uneasiness and moments of uncertainty you realize more than ever that you need God.

Stature does not assure favor among men. To walk in Kingdom stature as a High Priest, greater grace is needed. God will ensure your reserves are full. Your eyes will be opened to heavenly secrets and ancient pathways, and you'll gain wisdom and discernment to navigate dimensions and realms of the spirit. The key is to maintain stature in the midst of the most adverse pressures. God gives you grace to do it. Sometimes you will receive dishonor from men despite an honorable standing with God, or because of it. God asked Job to brace himself like a man, and He asks the same of you.

The prophet Jeremiah endured beatings and prison because he spoke the truth (Jeremiah 37). He had grace to endure. Paul and Silas were beaten after they cast an evil spirit out of a young woman (Acts 16). They had grace to endure. Peter was imprisoned because of his faith (Acts 12). He had grace to endure. Jeremiah's favor manifested when King Zedekiah removed him from prison to inquire secretly about a word from the Lord (Jeremiah 37). Paul and Silas experienced grace when God shook the foundations of the prison where they were incarcerated and opened all the doors (Acts 16). In Peter's case, an angel led him out of prison in answer to the prayers of the saints (Acts 12).

The grace bestowed to these servants of God helped them through severe persecution, and they found greater favor with Him. Expect His favor to lead you from one dimension of purpose to another, from one level of spiritual maturity to another. Look to Him in the midst of persecution; for there is much work to do in the Kingdom. Prepare yourself for assignments that fulfill purpose.

Commissions Divine Appointments

In the Old Testament divinely appointed assignments were initiated by God, then commissioned by one of His trusted servants, usually a prophet or priest. Jehu was anointed king by a designee sent from the prophet Elisha, in an inner room. He was commissioned by God to destroy Jezebel and the entire lineage of King Ahab (2 Kings 9:1-3). King David was anointed by the prophet Samuel when he was still a young shepherd boy on the mountain side. It took place in his home, among family. David was commissioned by God to govern Israel (1 Samuel 16:11-13). King Saul was also privately anointed by Samuel (1 Samuel 9 & 10).

Many wish to be anointed publicly. They seek recognition and notoriety to validate the anointing. They wait for individuals to lay hands upon them, believing that is how it is attained. There is no concern about whether God has anointed them for a particular purpose, or whether he has validated them. This is dangerous because all anointings come directly from God.

Reinhard Bonnke states,

> Scripturally ... there is no such thing as an anointing, only
> *the* anointing—the anointing of the Holy Spirit or baptism
> with the Spirit. *Holy Spirit* anointing is fully scriptural. In
> the Old Testament all who served God had to be anointed.
> This is replaced in the New Testament by the Holy Spirit—
> given for all believers. "Anointing" is just one of the
> synonyms for the baptism in the Spirit used in Scripture.[1]

It is the Holy Spirit anointing that you want, but He
cannot rest on a contaminated vessel. He cannot use someone
who will merely infect rather than affect others.

The anointing must come from God. In order to receive and
operate in it, make sure you are continually connected to the
source of its power. He chooses and calls, He prepares and
commissions. Jehu, Paul and David were all anointed, but none
were infallible. They made mistakes, but were not defined by
those mistakes. David consistently purged himself and righted
wrongs. He removed contaminants so he could continue being a
vessel God would use. The same is required of you. Remain
pure and contrite so the anointing can rest on you.

The anointing is not a feeling. It is present when the Holy
Spirit comes and equips those who are called to handle divine
assignments. Bonnke mentions David's anointing to destroy
Goliath and Samson's anointing to destroy the Philistines as
examples of anointings not felt, but rather activated when they
began to do what God equipped them to:

> The anointing is for all believers, for all are to serve. We
> are "a royal priesthood" (1 Pet. 2:9). Note carefully, though,
> that anointing is not a kind of emotional pleasure. It comes
> into activity when we serve.
>
> Any strong man does not feel his strength while sitting
> down; he feels it only when he exerts himself. David did
> not feel anointed in any particular sense, but when he
> faced Goliath he knew he was. Samson became strong only

when he went into action for God, for it was then that the Spirit of God came upon him (Judg. 14:6).[1]

Every provision to fulfill destiny is available because of the anointing. There are times you may feel the presence of God, but the anointing will draw the glory of His *Manifest Presence*. That glory brings miracles, signs and wonders. It creates atmospheres and avenues for God to use you in ways you never imagined. Jehu was physically equipped to confront Jezebel, but without an activation of the anointing, her Eunuchs would not have willingly consented to assist him in destroying her. The power of Jehu's anointing unwittingly caused them to help in fulfilling his purpose.

When the anointing is from God, His presence safeguards it. In Exodus thirty-three, God told Moses to take the people and go into the land He had promised to take them into. He offered to send Angels, but He would not go with them. Moses responded, "If your Presence does not go with us, do not send us from here" (vs. 15, NLT). Moses understood that although God had anointed him, they were powerless without His Presence.

You are anointed for purpose, but you must remain pure to maintain the integrity of that anointing. You do this by living a lifestyle of worship. The next chapter will look at the relationship between the oil and worship, as well as review the development of a life that has the capacity to draw the presence and magnify the anointing.

╫

Prayer

Father, teach me to position myself to be dressed; not only in an anointing, but also in Your grace. I desire more intimate encounters with You--to keep Your sound in my spirit; to do as You will. Teach me Your ways that I may walk in stature and become a spiritual Giant.

Give me strength and wisdom to withstand compression, without being affected by depression. I choose to Honor You in all that I do. I will walk, talk and live right according to Your Word.
In Jesus' Name, Amen.

Chapter Four

の

THE OIL AND WORSHIP

Worship is the greatest way to increase the level of the oil. There must be a constant flow to maintain an anointing. The Holy Spirit creates a catalyst that develops and presents the power into the atmosphere, into circumstances, into lives. Hands are laid, words are spoken and results are seen. Worship keeps the oil flowing abundantly.

The fragrance of worship begins an outpouring of the anointing oil upon your head, feet, lips, ears, and hands. When that oil touches you; the sweetness of God's presence fills your heart. It is a time of intimacy, communion, and fellowship. Your spirit receives sustenance and instruction straight from the Throne. There is a reverence for His Sovereign power as it rains the glory down upon you.

Your anointing has no real power without the presence of God. David prayed, "As the deer pants for streams of water, so my soul pants for you, my God. My soul thirsts for God, for the living God. Where can I go and meet with God?" (Psalm 42:1-2). This was a desperate longing for an intimate connection that could only be found in worship. Other things are found in it too; like peace, comfort and joy.

It is important to understand the power of the oil and appreciate the fragrance of its presence. Under the anointing, God will cause dynamic works to be manifested through you. He will do this as you reverently handle and nurture it. Don't be casual or careless about what He has imparted to you.

The oil initiates a strong connection to Daddy God, Abba Father, El-Shaddai, and makes room for the Comforter (the Holy Spirit) to dwell within you. You are in the secret place, behind the veil, where God reveals Himself and shares deep revelations that sometimes cause you to weep at their intensity. You long to stay, to live and breathe Him in with every second as you thirst for more of His presence.

The level of oil determines the level of power. When the flow is cut off and opportunities to display the power present themselves, there is no manifestation because there is no oil. No worship, no prayer, no relationship with God, equals no oil. While you are trying to restore your oil reserves there are those who need your anointing. Instead of experiencing it, they encounter a void. Think about the ten virgins in Matthew 25. The Bible says that, "five were foolish and five were wise" (vs. 2). The wise "took oil in jars along with their lamps" (vs. 4). They took time to prepare for the bridegroom's arrival. The five foolish virgins were not prepared for the inevitable.

They waited until it was too late, then tried to glean a portion of oil from the others who had taken the time to prepare, saying, "Give us some of your oil; our lamps are going out" (vs. 8). The response? "There may not be enough for both us and you. Instead, go to those who sell oil and buy some for yourselves" (vs. 9). There is a key lesson in that exchange. Do not lose your anointing because of others who are unwilling to take the time to develop their own relationship with God and press in for their oil. A lifestyle of worship builds oil reserves, develops a stronger anointing and draws greater spiritual power.

If you are not plugged into the Holy Spirit, you could find yourself in the same position as the five foolish virgins: dry and powerless (Matthew 25:10). They missed the opportunity to experience the glory. The realization that this is possible can produce feelings of desolation and hopelessness. If you have missed the opportunity; do not sink into despair. Carve out special time to spend with the Lord. Repent, get into His Word and His Presence and oil will begin to flow.

The foolish virgins were not positioned for a sustained flow of the anointing. Instead of keeping their eyes open for the coming of the bridegroom, they slept. They had no reserve oil to begin with, yet they slept. While they were sleeping, the oil in the lamps burned out until the light died. Darkness became their new reality. They had distress, not assurance.

When you are adorned in worship, distress and anxiety cannot rest on you. Worship literally drapes over your Spirit. It makes it impossible for the devil to gain footholds or breach spiritual territory.

When Jesus heard Lazarus was dead, He did not become anxious or hasty. He knew the power within Him would work because of His devotion to and constant communion with His Father. It was a relationship fostered in prayer which produced the overflow of oil in His life.

At Lazarus' tomb, he spoke plainly, "Father, I thank you that you have heard me. I knew that you always hear me, but I said this for the benefit of the people standing here, that they may believe that you sent me." Jesus called in a loud voice, "Lazarus, come out!"(John 11:41-43). There was no worry, no fear, no anxiety, just an assurance that what He asked would manifest.

The anointing does not descend suddenly. What have you gone through? What pain have you endured? Have you suffered mistreatment or been gravely misunderstood? What price are you paying to carry the anointing? The trials and tests you endure serve a greater purpose. You may feel embattled and broken all at the same time, but hold on. God is shaping you for destiny. Never take your journey lightly.

The concept of having to pay a price to be made is not new. Read the accounts of the lives of David, Joseph, Paul, Peter, John, Elisha, and many who were processed through pain. They were elevated in affliction, and anointed in the midst of it all. The process is sometimes arduous, but the reward is great. Jesus paid too, and He is the Son of God.

When individuals circumvent the process that draws the oil, they encounter the process again. Sometimes they are already in the midst of ministry when this happens. Many do not have an opportunity to run away like Elijah did (1 Kings

19). Instead they sing through the pain, preach and teach through the pain, pray and prophesy through the pain, all while needing encouragement themselves.

On the other hand, there are those who step into ministry prematurely and end up helping to facilitate the "spiritual death" of many. When Moses killed the Egyptian he lost the trust of the people he was supposed to deliver and ran into the wilderness (Exodus 2).

The woman who poured the fragrant oil upon Jesus' head knew she was deemed unworthy in the eyes of men. She may have even struggled with the thought of whether or not Jesus Himself could have a low opinion of her. Others criticized her terribly, but the desire to honor Christ was more than the focus on her limitations or words of the critics. As a matter of fact, she did get Jesus' attention. He defended her and honored her among the people (Matthew 26:10, 13). Her devotion and worship left an indelible impression. Stay humble and plugged in. Don't allow anything or anyone to limit or disrupt your time with God.

Oil saturation comes through consecration. You must actively demonstrate that you are truly committed to developing a strong relationship with God. The expression of devotion is a conduit that opens and controls the flow of the oil in your life. Reduced oil flow lessens the ability to maintain a sanctified and anointed walk and ministry.

Holiness is a precursor if you want to be used by God; but no one can compel you to seek it. If the flow begins to slow and ebb, you are solely responsible. There is no one you can hold accountable.

WALK IN HOLINESS

Daniel prayed despite the threat of imminent death because he chose to live a holy life without reservation or compromise (Daniel 6:10). He was forced to endure a Babylonian system that had no respect for His God, but he did not allow that Babylonian system to come alive in him.

Holiness will draw both friends and enemies. A decision to live holy will cause some to war with you. Hebrews 12:14 says, "Follow peace with all men, and holiness, without which no man shall see the Lord" (KJV). That does not always work simply because it is your heart's desire.

Daniel's Babylonian counterparts plotted to kill him because he chose to stand (Daniel 6). He was not fighting against them, yet they wanted him dead. His stance also garnered allies. The King was drawn to Daniel because he was righteous. Although he was duped by his satraps into putting him in danger, it was his desire to save Daniel's life. The King could not rest until he knew he was safe (Daniel 6:17-23).

The Psalmist David asked, "Lord, who shall dwell [temporarily] in Your tabernacle? Who shall dwell [permanently] on Your holy hill?" (Psalm 15:1, AMP). He answered, "He who walks and lives uprightly and blamelessly, who works rightness and justice and speaks and thinks the truth in his heart" (Psalm 14:2, AMP).

Living blamelessly does not mean you will never be in error. What is your heart's attitude when you find yourself in that place? Are you immediately repentant? Are you willing to do what is required to maintain purity of heart and purpose?

It is not a struggle to live a holy life. Your walk, speech and heart work in tandem to secure a position on God's holy hill. You can live there with the help of the Holy Spirit. You simply need to invite Him in and remain accurately connected in order to clearly hear what He is saying. Be willing and obedient to His will.

In Exodus 30:25-29 and Exodus 40:9, Moses is commanded to anoint the tabernacle and its furnishings so "that they may be most holy." In the Old Testament, the building and priestly rituals were the conduit to God; but the sacrifice of God's Son, Jesus, has given you direct access to the Throne Room. You are the tabernacle, the holy temple (1 Corinthians 6:19). You can enter the holy of holies without ceremony (Hebrews 10:19-20).

A holy walk is a safeguard, ushered in through a lifestyle of worship. The power of the blood, a yielded heart, prayer, worship, faith and conviction give you access to the presence of Jehovah. If you dwell there, He will walk with you and talk to you about some of the most significant things you'll hear this side of Heaven. You are not looking for intermittent worship, but a lifestyle of worship, which is stimulated and increased when you develop a spirit of worship.

THE SPIRIT OF WORSHIP

You cannot ask a Sovereign God to dwell in a ritual. He will not be touched by a shallow offering of worship. It is not a genuine invitation to His holy presence. The woman of Samaria told Jesus, "Our ancestors worshiped on this mountain, but you Jews claim that the place where we must worship is in Jerusalem" (John 4:20). Jesus replied,

> Woman... believe me, a time is coming when you will worship the Father neither on this mountain nor in Jerusalem...a time is coming and has now come when the true worshipers will worship the Father in the Spirit and in truth, for they are the kind of worshipers the Father seeks. God is spirit, and his worshipers must worship in the spirit and in truth (John 4:23-24).

Notice, Jesus said, *in the spirit and in truth.* An authentic worshipper's heart's desire to invite and actually spend intimate time with God will draw Him. Someone merely meeting daily self imposed quotas, like reading a number of biblical chapters per day, or spending a certain amount of minutes in prayer (with no real spiritual engagement) is the exact opposite of those whom God seek.

There is no truth in outward displays of worship by a vessel that is contaminated. Empty displays will never yield results, instead an infiltration of the soul and spirit by enemy designed toxins repel the Holy Spirit. Jesus spoke against pharisaical displays, which are blatant lies; they are overtly empty, hypocritical exhibitions, mere charades (Matthew 23:25-28).

The appearance of a clean outside, with a rotten, dirty inside makes one an unsuitable habitation for the Holy Spirit. Worship must be genuine. Pure hearts should speak volumes about who God is, and what He means to those who take time to lay themselves on the horns of the altar (Psalms 118:27).

If the Holy Spirit cannot dwell in you, you will not live in a spirit of worship. In Matthew fifteen, Jesus quotes Isaiah saying, "These people honor me with their lips, but their hearts are far from me" (vs. 8). That is the state of someone who does not worship in spirit and in truth. God is the creator, sustainer and lifter of your head. He is a rock, strength and shield, your deliverer. He is the beginning and ending. God deserves the honor of true worship.

True worship is not religious. It is an expression of pure love, without reservation, hesitation or expectation. Mary poured out from the alabaster box, not considering the cost of the oil, not taking into account her reputation; not thinking of the consequences she would endure from those in her community. She did not consider herself at all. She thought of the God who meant so much to her, and gave her most precious and her best. There was no pride or desire for the attention she received. She simply wanted to worship with heart and soul. She gained from it, but not because she sought recognition.

You benefit from living a worship lifestyle. God does not desire worship because He seeks adulation. He wants to see you in a place of heightened spiritual connection and dominion, where you can feel Him and know without a shred of doubt what He is speaking to you. He wants you to prosper in all areas of your life. He wants you to know His unconditional love. God wants you to have great joy and the power of His Spirit.

The oil that is poured is not intended to remain confined, rather it is meant to be poured out to others. Only as you pour out is there room for fresh oil to fill you again. In the story of the widow's olive oil in Second Kings chapter four, Elisha asked the widow to go around and ask neighbors for empty jars (vs. 3). He knew the small jar of oil in her possession was about to be magnified exponentially because of her obedience. After she gathered vessels, he requested she go inside, close the door, and begin to pour into them. She was not doing it as an act to publicly display the miraculous, she was simply being obedient.

In order to receive a constant flow of oil in your life, you must be willing to pour out that which is poured into you solely to draw others into the Kingdom. The Bible says, "The oil stayed" (2 Kings 4:4-6, KJV), but only after all of the vessels had been filled. Naturally, she sold the oil for profit; but the oil of anointing God pours out is priceless. Anyone seeking personal gain from it will experience a loss of authenticity and power.

A true worshipper does not count the cost. Mary had a speechless conversation with Jesus as she made her way to Him, but He heard her, above the din, the criticism, the cynicism, and the cruel snickers. She pressed through people and her own feelings of shame and degradation to get to Jesus. She was driven to worship by a spirit of worship, which was compelling and unstoppable.

The spirit of worship creates a pure desire to commune with an audience of one. Adam was not yet formed when God created the heavens and earth but through relationship, he came to know the nature and power of God, which is why after he tasted the forbidden fruit; he hid from the one who, until then, had been everything to them (Genesis 3:8). Adam felt unworthy to be in the presence of that power and love. He was ashamed to stand in God's Holiness.

Before he sinned, Adam had phenomenal God encounters which empowered him to be all he was created to be, but he lost focus and gave place to another [Lucifer]. Adam allowed one who was self serving, prideful and diabolical to displace him from dimensions he had already received from God. It was the greatest mistake of his life. Adam and Eve stopped the flow of the anointing oil when they listened to the serpent and responded favorably to his crafty suggestions.

Jesus brought redemption. He knew the power in living a completely God-focused life. This was evident in the daily expression of His relationship with His Father. It was evident in His devotional time and resulting God given power. It was evident in the out working of that power. Everywhere He went transformation happened. Jesus worshipped God with His life.

That is the level of commitment required to draw the potency and efficiency of the oil.

Christ's blood has given you the ability to draw both the oil and its power. He said, "Very truly I tell you, whoever believes in me will do the works I have been doing, and they will do even greater things" (John 14:12). Remaining saturated in the oil positions you to display great power also, but you must first believe.

THE SPIRIT OF CHRIST

One key facet to Christ's success as a Son was the fact that He unfalteringly believed in the power of the oil. There was absolutely no doubt in His heart. That belief caused His focus to be directed solely toward purpose. There were no *what ifs* to distract; no *if onlys* to dissuade. It was all about Daddy God and fulfilling the call on His life.

Jesus allowed the oil to completely drench Him. He submitted Himself to an oversupply of the anointing. He produced wondrous works in His Father's name, all the while humbly acknowledging the true source of power.

He said, "When you have lifted up the Son of Man, then you will know that I am he and that I do nothing on my own but speak just what the Father has taught me" (John 8:28). The oil He drew embodied and transmitted the authority of Heaven. No one had the power to keep it from working.

You have access to this same oil, and you can receive the same anointing. Remember, Jesus declared you would do even greater works than He did (John 14:12). This is only possible when you function as a true Christ follower. You have to walk, talk, and act like Him. That includes building a strong relationship with God by plugging in (praying, praising, worshipping, reading the Word continually and living according to its precepts), thereby dwelling in a place of constant power and favor.

POWER & FAVOR

At an early age, God's favor was seen on the child Jesus. When He was days old, the Shepherds saw it. It was seen by Simeon, a man of faith and devotion and also by the Prophet Anna. In the case of the Shepherds, it occurred at the time of His birth as they were keeping watch. Simeon and Anna observed it when baby Jesus was being purified on the eighth day, as was their cultural custom.

Purity and devotion open the gateway to revelation. Simeon's and Anna's devotion and pure lifestyle converged with the residue of the anointing on baby Jesus. It opened their spiritual eyes and delivered sure revelation that He was the long awaited Messiah who would be Savior (Luke 2:30-32). Simeon exalted Him; and Anna declared Him Redeemer of Israel (Luke 2:38).

Those who are casual in their pursuit of God rarely have opportunity to hear directly from Him, much less be trusted with Heavenly mysteries. Simeon was righteous, and the Spirit of God was upon him. It directed him to enter the Temple and revealed the spirit of Christ, all because Simeon had relationship with God. The scripture describes him as devout.

Anna, too, was full of the Presence—she lived with It. The place of God was her residence (Luke 2:37). She communed with Him and this qualified them both as trustworthy conduits to deliver God's revelatory Word about His Son to the people.

Jesus' parents observed and pondered all that was being said by everyone. I imagine Mary often wondered throughout Jesus' lifetime; "Lord, what have I done to deserve this honor; this challenge, this wonderful thing? Why was I found worthy?" I believe she prayed, "Oh Lord, give me what it takes to nurture and impart to this Your Son." Both Mary *and* Joseph were in awe of their responsibility, and they "marveled at what was said about him [Jesus]" (Luke 2:33). It was a sobering experience, but "they did all that was required by God's law...Jesus grew, became strong and the grace of God was upon Him" (Luke 2:39-40).

Power brings favor, favor draws power. When either power or favor are present, persecutors lie in wait seeking to disrupt, disallow, desecrate and destroy. This was true, even for Jesus. Many felt threatened by His anointing and its power. He exuded it just by being, while they sought it by doing. They could not understand the ease with which Jesus operated in dimensions which were inaccessible to them. The futility and unattainability of what they sought drove them mad, causing them to eventually inflict horrific acts of persecution upon Him. They were looking for power, not understanding it could only be gained through the anointing.

PERSECUTION, DEATH & RESURRECTION

Jesus lived as a man. His humanity made Him vulnerable but that vulnerability could not diminish the anointing. Constant scrutiny, rejection and persecution caused Him to get even closer to His Father. They did not weaken Him. Instead He spent more time in prayer and increased in stature and power. He was disowned, mocked, and spat upon. The flesh was torn from His body and a crown of thorns pushed deeply into His brow. They pierced His side, and He was taunted even in suffering. His tormentors could not wait for Him to die.

They saw His power revealed while He was on the cross, and afterwards in the spirit driven works of His disciples. They imagined that power would automatically be theirs once Jesus was gone, but were at a loss when they realized this would not be so.

Now there were more people to crucify; more to wipe out in order to try and gain the power they sought. They did not understand that Jesus willingly laid His life down, or anticipate the ultimate expression of love which converted hearts on the cross *and* at the foot of the cross after His death. Despite all that was preached throughout His ministry, they were still shocked when anointed power manifested because they never believed Jesus was truly God's Son.

In the Garden of Gethsemane, blood and sweat mixed as He agonized over what was before Him. On the cross, His side was pierced and blood and water flowed (John 19:33-34). But when he died, as complete obedience was fulfilled, something else began to take place. His declaration, "It is finished," was a signal both to Heaven and hell of what was to come (John 19:30).

When Jesus lifted His voice, the oil began flowing throughout the earth, into its deepest depths. It disrupted the historical structure and composition of hell. No longer did it have power over a Saint of God. The anointing of the oil and the blood converged to form an impenetrable barrier. It coated the depths of hades like a blanket as He descended, and sustained Him for three days while He conquered death and the grave. It fueled Him with greater power. The earth shook, and the veil which hindered mankind from having direct access to God was torn. Heaven responded resoundingly. Amazing and incredible things happened on Golgotha during and after the crucifixion.

Christ was buried and descended into Sheol, but when He rose from the dead the anointing propelled Him upward. It changed molecular structures on the way up, destroying natural boundaries to awaken even greater supernatural demonstrations. He walked through walls; translated from one location to another. He stood among men who knew him, yet they did not recognize Him. Death could not hold Him because He had become an even greater Power.

It was not the first time blood and oil were mixed together to create a purity Satan could not penetrate. In Leviticus eight, during the purification process of Aaron and his sons, "Moses took some of the anointing oil and some of the blood from the altar and sprinkled them on Aaron and his garments and on his sons and their garments...and consecrated Aaron and his garments and his sons and their garments" (vs. 30).

Once the blood and oil were sprinkled, Aaron and his sons were told to stay in the entrance of the tent of meeting for seven days (Leviticus 8:33-35) and "they did everything the Lord commanded through Moses" (Leviticus 8:36). That obedience caused the process of purification to be fulfilled, and they moved into their next phase of ministry with God's blessing. Clearly, obedience is a prerequisite for the power to manifest and for purity to repel darkness.

The same was true for Jesus. When His time on earth was done, He moved into the next phase, ascending into Heaven, to be "seated at the right hand of the Father also interceding for us" (Romans 8:34).

After the resurrection the Holy Spirit revealed Himself. He gave power to the disciples and many came to believe in Christ. In Acts 10:44-48 while Peter was yet speaking, the Holy Spirit came on all who heard the message, even the Gentiles and they were also baptized in Jesus' name. There was a magnification of the anointing on Peter's life - an anointing for souls and for transformation power to manifest. It brought authority, favor, privilege, and relationship. It was possible because of Jesus' life, death and resurrection.

As Jesus told the woman of Samaria; "If you drink of the water I give you, you shall never thirst again. It will become a spring of water welling up to eternal life" (John 4:14). He spoke of the same eternal life secured at Calvary. It is the hope of that eternal life which brings "joy unspeakable and full of glory" (1 Peter 1:8); a hope made possible by "the resurrection of Jesus from the dead" (1 Peter 1:3). To Him be "Blessing and honor and glory and power forever" (Revelations 5:13), your Lord, your God, your King.

JOY

You can receive the kind of joy David felt when "he brought the Ark up from Obed-Edom's house" (2 Samuel 6:12). The presence of God and the anointing over Jerusalem was cause for great jubilation. Joy made David remove his outer garments and dance with abandon in the streets. There was no self-consciousness. He was not concerned about how he would be perceived. This kind of behavior was unheard of -David, the King, dancing in the street in the ephod, any modicum of stately decorum thrown out the window as he worshipped.

David was not the only one filled with joy. "All the Israelites [also] shouted with joy and blew the trumpets as they brought the Ark of the LORD to the city" (2 Samuel 6:15). It was a time of unparalleled celebration.

The anointing will do that to you; saturate you with an

incomprehensible joy. It caused the Israelites to worship. Worship kept their heart and attitude in the right place, not downcast or disheartened, but uplifted and celebratory. Joy is a shield, a deflector, an insulator from negativity or anything that would compromise the anointing.

Joy keeps spirits free and accessible to God. It shields you from spiritual infections. Hebrews 1:9 says, "You have loved righteousness and hated wickedness; therefore God, your God, has set you above your companions by anointing you with the oil of joy." Nehemiah declared to the Israelites that "the joy of the Lord is strength" (Nehemiah 8:10). A spirit of joy holds you together like glue, even when things are falling apart around you. There is also joy in worship. As you exalt The King, it rises up in your heart and draws the oil into your life. A spirit of prayer also rises. God is listening. Talk to Him and watch things consistently shift from one dimension to the next.

THE THRESHING FLOOR

In First Chronicles twenty-one, King David allowed himself to be tempted, and conducted a census of Israel against God's will. It brought destruction to the nation. As David repented, he saw the Angel of the Lord, sword drawn, standing between Heaven and earth over the threshing floor of Araunah. He and his elders, prayed for the lives of the people to be spared, and he alone be held accountable. God responded, instructing David to build an altar on that threshing floor.

David wanted an intimate encounter, and he would not offer worship on someone else's threshing floor. He paid a great price for the privilege of building the altar, but insisted on paying because his desire was to make the necessary sacrifice to have a second chance to honor God. This scripture was significant to me. Because of it, I identify the threshing floor as a place of prayer, repentance, and intimate worship. It is a place to pound, sift and separate, a place of formation.

There, pressure is forcefully applied to wheat to prepare it for use. You not only talk to God on the threshing floor, but you allow Him to do what He will so great things may be accomplished through you. What better place to position yourself to receive the oil of anointing and the blessing of the Holy Spirit than a place of prayer?

In Second Chronicles eighteen, King Ahab (of Israel) and King Jehoshaphat (of Judah), were on the threshing floor at the gate of Samaria. Prophets prophesied that they would destroy the Arameans of Ramoth Gilead if they went into battle against them. King Ahab's life was not guided by God, therefore the prophets he listened to were not from God. It prompted King Jehoshaphat to ask, "Is there no longer a prophet of the Lord here whom we can inquire of?" (vs. 6). He understood that the word they needed should come directly from God, yet he followed King Ahab into a battle God specifically said would lead to Ahab's death. It was God's mercy on Jehoshaphat's life which spared him. He learned some tough lessons and came away understanding that:

On the threshing floor
1.   You must listen carefully; your hearing cannot be impaired.
2.   You will receive an accurate word directly from the Throne Room.
3.   Be ready and willing to accept and act upon true revelation from the Father.
4.   Allow your spirit to be discerning.
5.   Be obedient to the truths revealed on the threshing floor and avoid the consequences of disobedience.
6.   Be resolute in your decision to follow instructions; there can be no wavering.
7.   You will develop new resolve after the threshing floor.
8.   The threshing floor encounter stirs the true prophetic gift, but your spirit must be open to God (2 Chronicles 18:1-34).

These lessons had a sobering effect on King Jehoshaphat. He went back to Judah, resolving to set things in order. He was determined to serve, to position himself and those around him to hear the Word of the Lord and obey. The steps Jehoshaphat took were resolute. He appointed Priests and Levites over the people and said, "You must serve faithfully and wholeheartedly in the fear of the LORD" (2 Chronicles 19:9). He identified priorities, observed God's statutes and worshiped. He developed the right attitude toward God and communicated it to all the people.

Although Jehoshaphat had been on a threshing floor with King Ahab, it had no significance because both of their spirits were wrong. Their motives were wrong, and the initial source of their intel (lying prophets) was wrong.

Those prophets only sought to find favor in the eyes of King Ahab. They were men pleasers, not anointed messengers, who ignorantly spoke words that assured his death. King Ahab and King Jehoshaphat eventually heard from the true prophet of God, but had already decided to follow their own hearts on the matter. The principles of the threshing floor were never employed.

After the encounter, King Jehoshaphat found himself in a place of extreme humility and reverential fear. The next time he had to make a decision about going to war (2 Chronicles 20) he knew exactly what to do. He was in the Temple of the Lord, using key principles of the threshing floor. First he prayed to God, "We do not know what to do, but our eyes are on you" (vs. 12). Then he listened for an answer. One came almost immediately (vs. 14-17).

Jehoshaphat received the prophetic word and put a few more threshing floor principles into action. He discerned that the word was from God and led the people in worship and praise. He obeyed the word, which led to a rousing victory. While they were yet praising, the enemy was destroyed because God had anointed them for victory. When the battle was over, they went directly to the temple to worship (2 Chronicles 20:28).

If you want to be anointed to win, go to the threshing floor with the right attitude and the right tools. God will do the rest. Judah's enemies also developed a reverential fear for God. They knew they could not successfully contend with King Jehoshaphat if the anointing of God was his shield and strength. It kept peace in their city.

Jehoshaphat's earlier failures were due to a lack of respect for the threshing floor principles. When he appropriated the right principles, they were victorious. He saw the power the threshing floor exuded, both on those who misused it and those who respected it. There is no need for you to suffer because of a lack of understanding. Reverence God's presence during your phase of sifting.

Uzzah's irreverence caused him to die on Nacon's threshing floor because he inappropriately held the Ark (2 Samuel 6:6-7). His touch was casual. It was done instinctively, not considering the instructions God had given regarding how the Ark should be handled. It was a fatal error, and the consequence frightened King David.

How often are you on the threshing floor? Do you come unimpeded by wrong desires, distorted focus or bad attitudes? Are you willing to truly see God and hear from Him? If the answer is yes, humble yourself before you come to the Throne Room. Allow flesh to shrivel up and die as God's presence manifests. Seek Him first, desire and chase after the intimacy that opens your spiritual ears and eyes. Intimacy sensitizes accurate discernment. Listen keenly and be willing to obey the voice of God.

Jehoshaphat experienced grace on the threshing floor. Use him as a model. Don't forget Uzzah. Never become so familiar with the presence of God that you overlook honor and obedience. The threshing floor is a place of constant oil overflow and power. It is there for you. Enter into the holy place as often as you can. Your life will never be the same.

BEHIND THE VEIL

Oh the glory of that sacred place behind the veil. It feeds the spirit and enhances the soul. God reveals dimensions of Himself. The encounter opens ears to His voice and releases special understanding of hidden things. Ezekiel describes the radiant glory of the Presence, "The cloud filled the temple, and the court was full of the radiance of the glory of the LORD. The sound of the wings of the cherubim could be heard as far away as the outer court, like the voice of God Almighty when He speaks" (Ezekiel 10:4-5).

Moving toward purpose without the anointing is a bleak and futile journey. There is a dramatic deficit when one is called to serve but does not fulfill purpose. I can speak of this, because I have experienced it. It is a desolate moment to stand before God and be found wanting, unable to deliver more than just a performance, incapable of making an impact spiritually. It is a state that drives you to your knees, desiring to be filled up so you can pour out something of substance. Moses said to the Lord, "If your Presence does not go with us, do not send us up from here" (Exodus 33:15). I understand how he felt. I understand why he implored God to stay with them as they headed toward destiny.

The goal is to be like Jeremiah, even when your body and mind seek to sway you from serving. The power of the anointing and the presence of the Holy Spirit is like the Word he sought to trap in the shell of a spirit that wanted to run from purpose. Eventually, he confessed [of the Lord] "His Word is in my heart like a fire, a fire shut up in my bones. I am weary of holding it in; indeed I cannot" (Jeremiah 20:9). The fire could not be contained; it had to be free to burn. It drove Jeremiah. It compelled him to manifest the power of God through his gift.

The spirit of sacrifice keeps the power in your life. Willing yourself to do God's will sometimes seems impossible. It is an unpopular yet power-filled way of life. The call drives you to the altar, to the cross, to the Holy Place. You need to dwell there in order to find strength to wholeheartedly continue on the path to destiny. Look neither to the right or the left, but keep your eyes fixed on God. Find your place of worship and dwell there. Surrender completely.

The Old Testament Tabernacle was the place of worship, the Holy of Holies where only the sanctified could enter and be filled. They were destroyed by its power if there was contamination in their lives. Entrants prepared themselves for worship at the brazen altar where sacrifices were made for purification and atonement. They had to qualify to go behind the veil. Everything not like God had to be separated and purged. The area was so sacred, that entering with a tainted spirit meant certain death.

Never carelessly enter the Presence. Go before God with absolute meekness, observing and acknowledging His Sovereignty. Don't be complacent. If you do, your soul becomes barren, and Satan gains full access.

There are biblical examples of how the lives of those who allow the enemy entrance are changed. Servants like King Saul and Samson lost their anointing, and eventually their lives. David had a momentary slip and his entire family was affected. The oil is needed to keep the light of God visible and functional at all times. God told Moses,

> Command the Israelites to bring you clear oil of pressed olives for the light so that the lamps may be kept burning continually. Outside the curtain that shields the ark of the covenant law in the tent of meeting, Aaron is to tend the lamps before the LORD from evening till morning, continually. This is to be a lasting ordinance for the generations to come. The lamps on the pure gold lampstand before the LORD must be tended continually (Leviticus 24:1-4).

The oil in the lamps is constantly reduced by the continuously burning fire. To keep the lamps lit, more oil must be produced.

Moses lived behind the veil as he led the people out of Egypt. The glory resided with him at all times (Exodus 24:1-2). Living behind the veil fosters an unbreakable covenant with the Holy Spirit. Moses' covenant relationship with God qualified him for close encounters, deep revelations and strategy. It made him eligible to be God's conduit to the people. He was the mouthpiece who commanded the nation's enemies as instructed by the Lord.

Jesus is behind the veil. You have a hope, an anchor for the soul. Enter the inner sanctuary; Jesus lives there. This knowledge warms my heart. His Presence surrounds me. Even when I cannot feel Him, I know that He is there, and I worship. Those who embrace His love and the promise of eternal life willingly and frequently go behind the veil, because there is direct access to Him (Hebrews 6:17-20).

Dwell behind the veil. Increase the opportunity to become more like Jesus, to know more about Him, to surrender your heart completely. Position yourself to hear. Receive a stronger anointing. It magnifies the flow of the oil in your life. Walk in holiness and let the joy of the Lord be your strength. As you press in, you will move into greater dimensions to glorify God and share the gospel of the Kingdom.

Prayer

Dear Heavenly Father, My desire is for righteousness to rule. Drape me in the Spirit of Christ as I press toward the mark. I don't want to fail you Lord, or fail those you've assigned to me. Let me be a vessel fit for use, blessed with power and might, filled with grace and favor. I hunger for holiness and for the high calling. I thirst for You.

I understand that sometimes I may endure affliction, and I will not dwell in vain glory. Lord, carry me when I need to be carried, compel change if I ever become careless. Father, help me to walk in the Spirit, In Jesus' name, Amen.

Chapter Five

❧

THE KINGLY ANOINTING

God has called His people as kings, prophets and priests to command His will into this earth realm. He equipped them to stand in the gap to initiate kingdom transformation. They must accurately represent Him to the world; preaching, teaching and manifesting the gospel so others may know Him. This assignment is not for the faint hearted. It will not be accomplished if you are polluted by contaminants. It takes a pure anointing to advance the Kingdom, but when a vessel is polluted it destroys, delays and infects others. Each calling is vital to the success of the mission. Let us take a look at the kingly anointing.

The kingly anointing demands the full attention, excellence, attentiveness, care, compassion, wisdom, understanding and knowledge of the king as a ruler. It is not an anointing that is bestowed upon many. A king provides protection and provision for his Kingdom. He is responsible for the well being of every subject.

Is he strong? Is he wise? Can he defend the territory? Is he compassionate? Is he respected throughout the kingdom and beyond? Is he loyal? It takes special character and fortitude to shoulder the responsibility.

To carry the anointing you are literally called to sacrifice the pursuit of personal goals. Never take it lightly because you can irresponsibly drive others toward hell by being unwilling to carry out God's commands. Abandon self pity and the desire for self preservation when persecution comes, like King David did when King Saul sought to slay him. He wanted to preserve his life, but understood the need to remain God centered and purpose focused.

A pure anointing does not pursue self agenda. While Saul was after him, David was not free. He became a fugitive, constantly looking over his shoulder. He had no real home, but he had a Kingdom mindset. David preserved the life of King Saul to please God. By doing so, he secured his position as heir to the throne (1 Samuel 24). He was driven to fulfill purpose.

Jesus paid the ultimate price. He gave up physical and emotional comfort to maintain His Kingly character and anointing. His reputation was tarnished and His entire life affected, yet devotion to Kingdom purpose took precedence. In the Garden of Gethsemane He said, "Father, if you are willing, take this cup from me; yet not my will, but yours be done" (Luke 22:42). The sacrifice sometimes felt unbearable, yet He knew it was not about Him. He humbled himself and willingly died for mankind.

In man's uprisings, and during the commission of the grossest sin, Christ rules. His rule subdued the kingdom of darkness and the kingdoms of the world to secure hope for you. He has all power and authority. There is nothing that can counter the expression of His righteous power. You have freedom to choose, and you are in control of your destiny. Control and authority to govern are two entirely different things.

ANOINTED TO RULE

You were anointed to rule when God told Adam to "be fruitful and multiply; fill the earth and subdue it; have dominion over the fish of the sea, over the birds of the air, and over every living thing that moves on the earth" (Genesis 1:28, NKJV). Ruling is in your DNA (Genesis 1:26), but ruling without the anointing introduces perversion. Dictatorships are formed. People are oppressed and depressed. That is the nature of

Satan, not the nature of Christ. It is imperative that your rule functions under the anointing of God's initial command.

Anointed Kings are made by God. "Are you the king of the Jews?' asked Pilate. "You have said so," Jesus replied" (Luke 5:2). Jesus was affirmed by His Father (Matthew 3:17), but immediately following that affirmation was tested (Matthew 4:1). While this may seem difficult to understand, this is how truly anointed Kings are made. They are often shaped in adversity, through wilderness experiences. There is a qualifying process; they must be proven.

The responsibilities of an anointed king are diverse both in nature and in degree of difficulty. Some affect the king only, while others affect the culture and success of the entire kingdom. The outcome is a direct result of the king's level of obedience to God's will and mandate for that kingdom.

An individual called to function in the kingly anointing will persevere until they fully embrace purpose. Saul was anointed by Samuel, yet there were several things he was asked to do before actually being crowned king (1 Samuel 10). David was also anointed by Samuel, yet went back to tending his sheep (1 Samuel 16).

Rising into the position of kingship after having been anointed is a process that sometimes requires tearing down the existing kingdom in order to accurately establish the pattern revealed by God. David faced and defeated the Philistine giant Goliath (1 Samuel 17). Then he ran from King Saul, who wanted to kill him (1 Samuel 18 & 19).

Anointed kings are called to do battle. Kings must go to battle to keep the kingdom safe and to expand it. A valiant fight displays strength and boosts influence in the nation and in surrounding regions. It speaks volumes to the rest of the world, often deterring other kingdoms from initiating military action.

Anointed kings destroy the legacy of contaminated kings. Jehu was called, positioned, poised, equipped and ready to destroy Ahab and Jezebel. The call was issued immediately after he was anointed. His purpose and steps to fulfill it were precise, annihilate a perverted king, queen, and their lineage, in order to bring God's order back to the kingdom (2 Kings 9:6-10).

Jehu's first task was to eliminate leaders who had been ruling Israel with fear and evil acts. There could be no residue of that legacy. It had to be obliterated. It was important that Jehu's spirit be completely open to God's leading. He had to be bold. He could not allow fear to grip him.

Anointed kings must be courageous. The spirit of intimidation had no control over Jehu. When he finally got to Jezreel, though Jezebel spoke, he was not moved by her words. He addressed angelic hosts in the realm of the spirit to speak to those under her command, and they were willing to become a part of God's new move for the kingdom (2 Kings 9:30-33).

Jezebel's actions and words showed a conflict of emotions. On one hand she sought to disarm Jehu with her intimidating character as she had no doubt often done with others before (2 Kings 9:30). On the other hand, her words showed fear and false bravado. Her thought might easily have been, "If he was bold enough to kill my sons, with seemingly no fear of reprisal; what on earth is he planning to do to me?" She did not issue a threat as she was prone to do; instead she asked a question "Have you come in peace?" (2 Kings 9:31). The question was also laced with the accusation: "You murderer of your master" (2 Kings 9:31), but it did not deter Jehu.

God shared a strategy with Jehu, which showed His wisdom in the matter. The first step was to remove Jezebel's heirs who were already kings (2 Kings 9:14-28). That sent a message to Jezebel: "I do not fear you. I will follow the commands of God and I am ready to destroy you." It told Jezebel's supporters that it would be a mistake to oppose Jehu.

It was important that he first discern who would help to fulfill God's command; then issue the directive to execute it. Jehu was focused and effectively prepared because a fresh anointing had been poured upon him.

Anointed kings rule by succession. When the kingly anointing is bestowed; it cannot be hijacked. Adonijah tried to take Solomon's throne. It was a crucial and deadly mistake. Often, scripture about Old Testament kings indicate that when a patriarch died the son (heir) took the throne. On occasion, those hungry for power or seeking revenge try to take the throne, not considering the fact they had not been anointed to rule.

That is exactly what Absalom did when he positioned himself at the side of the road leading to the gate of the city and enticed citizens of his father's kingdom. He wanted the honor that was due David. To the citizens of the Kingdom, he seemed genuinely concerned about their well being. He masked his disloyal desire as an overture of good will (2 Samuel 15:2-6). Once the people began to view him as a source of their solutions, Absalom lied to his father and left the kingdom. He began planning an offensive on David from the outside. This is not the kind of battle the anointed fight. Kings who use these tactics to gain position suffer severe consequences.

God anoints those He trusts to perform specific functions. They carry out His will for the region to which they are assigned. Absalom could have been on the throne of David, but his heart was angry and bitter. He harbored murderous thoughts, and a vengeful spirit. It was his only incentive to get up every morning. He devised schemes to lie and cheat his way to being ruler. God would not allow hypocritical, murderous intent to follow David's rule. It would utterly destroy the people.

David selected Solomon to succeed him. After all, he was the one commissioned to build the Tabernacle of the Lord. King David secured the required materials, but Solomon was anointed to take the throne and complete the task.

Anointed kings are called to bring peace. Kings must know when to fight and when to make peace. Solomon would not only build the Temple, but would also usher in an extended realm of peace in the nation. During his reign, God gave complete rest to the children of Israel. Solomon's leadership was exemplary. His God-centered resolve drew other nations to come and see what God had done.

One very popular example was the account of two mothers fighting over one child (1 Kings 3:16-28). While many refer to it when speaking of his wisdom, it also shows how his spirit of peace diffused what could have become an ongoing battle. That peace would not have been realized with Absalom on the throne.

Anointed kings know their enemy. Those carrying the kingly anointing must know how to first guard themselves, and by extension, the citizens of their Kingdom. One way of doing this is to accurately identify enemies and friends. King Hezekiah had a challenge in this area. He allowed the Prince of Babylon to get a look at all the treasures that were stored in the Temple.

Before the visit, the Prince sent letters and gifts during Hezekiah's illness. Because of this Hezekiah incorrectly identified him as a friend. When the Prince arrived, "Hezekiah received the envoys and showed them all that was in his storehouses—the silver, the gold, the spices and the fine olive oil—his armory and everything found among his treasures. There was nothing in his palace or in all his kingdom that Hezekiah did not show them" (2 Kings 20:13). It was a classic error, because at a later time, the Babylonians raided the Kingdom, took all the treasure and held the people captive.

Contaminated kings reveal kingdom secrets. Contaminated kings form wrong alliances which jeopardize the well being and safety of everyone in their Kingdom. What King Hezekiah thought was a gesture of goodwill was actually a tool used by Babylon to expand their kingdom at Israel's expense. Shortly after his gross error in judgment, Isaiah prophesied,

> The time will surely come when everything in your palace, and all that your predecessors have stored up until this day, will be carried off to Babylon. Nothing will be left, says the LORD. And some of your descendants, your own flesh and blood who will be born to you, will be taken away, and they will become eunuchs in the palace of the king of Babylon (2 Kings 20:17-18).

Hezekiah's actions fed the Babylonians desire to have his kingdom's treasures.

Contaminated kings do not fully yield to God. Jehoshaphat followed all the ways of the Lord but there was one thing that he held on to; he kept worshipping in the high places, offering incense to other gods (I Kings 22:43). How can one maintain focus on the mandates and purposes of God when they are worshipping idols? The Bible clearly states, "No man can serve two masters" (Matthew 6:24, KJV). King Asa was mindful of this when he "Took away the altars of the strange gods, and the high places, and brake down the images...Also he took away out of all the cities of Judah the high places and the images: and the kingdom was quiet before him" (2 Chronicles 14:3,5). He did not compromise or allow anyone to dishonor the Lord, not even his own flesh and blood (1 Kings 15:13). Asa's commitment to God was uncompromising.

Contaminated kings are disloyal. They illegally seize territory. In Judges nine, Abimelek who was a son of his father's female slave, murdered seventy of his brothers to gain access to the throne. He annihilated those he saw as competition and was crowned king. Within three years, the people he ruled began to rise up against him. He eventually died at their hands (vs. 57). God always vindicates His people.

Contaminated kings actively seek false prophecies to support perverted decisions. They relentlessly challenge the prophetic word. The primary goal is to discredit any prophet who speaks an accurate word which goes against what they desire to do. In Second Kings chapter one, King Ahaziah sent his messengers to consult a false god (Baal-Zebub, god of Ekron) about his health. How could an Israelite king believe that a graven image held the answer to his future? God responded by sending Elijah with a pronouncement of his death. The answer was swift and final (2 Kings 1:16-17).

Ahaziah's father (King Ahab) also had a blatant disrespect and disregard for the prophetic word and lost his life as well. Pride blinded them to the truth. As King Jehoshaphat advised,

"Believe in the LORD your God; so shall ye be established.
Believe His prophets; so shall ye prosper" (2 Chronicles 20:20).

Disbelieving the prophetic word does not make it untrue.
What it does do is position you for an outcome that is likely
detrimental. It affects you and those connected to you for
generations to come. Do not disregard the prophetic word.

Contaminated kings do not reverence the prophetic word.
Ahaziah was supremely arrogant. He kept trying to command
Elijah to his court despite the fact that the men sent to
commandeer Elijah never returned. Undoubtedly, this king
knew they were being consumed by God's fire at Elijah's word,
yet still believed somehow the next group would intimidate
Elijah. This displayed not only a lack of respect for both the
authority and the word of God, but also a certain disdain for
his prophet. When the third Captain, convinced of the power of
Elijah's God, humbled himself and pleaded for his life, an
Angel released Elijah to go to the King (2 Kings 1:9-15).

Contaminated kings alter the path of their seed. Saul was
Israel's first king. His reign started right, but it quickly
spiraled into something God never intended. His heart became
perverted, twisted by pride and jealousy. Who he was as a
result was not someone his son Jonathan wished to emulate.
The nature of the man he was destined to succeed repelled
Jonathan, and instead, drew him to David.

Saul's entire legacy died alongside him in battle. The
lineage ended and a new one began with King David. Because
Saul allowed his soul to become contaminated, Jonathan never
sat on the throne. Had he kept his anointing pure, Jonathan's
life may have been different.

Contaminated kings leave a contaminated legacy. You live
what you learn, and you become what you live. This principle
was no different for Old Testament kings whose predecessors
were contaminated. They could leave nothing but a tainted
legacy, passing down the tenets by which they lived to their
heirs. I mentioned King Ahab in an earlier chapter. His sons
displayed their father's lifestyle throughout their own lives.

Ahaziah was a key example, and he met the same fate as his father. He lived what he learned and suffered dire consequences (1 Kings 22:51-53).

Honorable lives produce good seeds. Take King Josiah, David's son. At a mere eight years-old he began ruling and "He did what was right in the eyes of the LORD and followed completely the ways of his father David, not turning aside to the right or to the left" (2 Kings 22:2).

Years before Josiah's reign, God referred to David as "a man after His [God's] own heart" (Acts 13:22), and in 2 Kings 22, that same "type" of heart is displayed by his son. He identified error, sought the face of God, repented and effected change. God's response to Josiah reflected how He felt about the choices Josiah made. He said,

> Because your heart was responsive and you humbled yourself before the LORD when you heard what I have spoken against this place and its people—that they would become a curse and be laid waste—and because you tore your robes and wept in my presence, I also have heard you, declares the LORD. Therefore I will gather you to your ancestors, and you will be buried in peace. Your eyes will not see all the disaster I am going to bring on this place (2 Kings 22:19-20).

Eighteen years into his reign, King Josiah discovered that The Book of the Law was found in the Temple. Once he read it and realized the nation had not been following the precepts it contained, Josiah took immediate action. He first consulted the prophet, Huldah (2 Kings 22) so he could hear God's heart on the matter.

Mercy was extended because Josiah had both a pure spirit and a contrite heart. His actions demonstrated life principles that King David exhibited after he committed adultery and murder. When confronted, David not only repented, but he also accepted the consequence of his actions and turned to worshipping God (2 Samuel 12:1-22).

God asks that you repent and ask forgiveness as soon you are aware of sin in your life. He knows you are not faultless, and has made provision for fallibility. Man needs help to maneuver through life's pathways. God sent His Son to die on the cross to defeat death and make redemption possible.

He provided His Word as a guide, a road map, to show you how to live a consecrated life. He provided weaponry to repel, withstand, and triumph over attacks of the enemy.

The Word contains keys to walk in victory and maintain a covering of grace (Ephesians 6:11 – 13).

Put on the armor of God; it never fails. In the next section I want to look at each piece in the context of the Kingly anointing and how it safeguards a Kingdom.

THE ARMOR

It is impossible to accurately operate in the kingly anointing without the right armor. There are key pieces which protect vital parts of the body, and crucial regions of vulnerability that require extra protection. Paul highlights them in Ephesians six. Even more notable than the pieces of armor are the areas they safeguard. I will discuss them in detail and identify the organs that become secure if you walk out the door covered in full gear daily. God considered the interconnectedness of organs and intricately designed your framework. He wants both your spiritual and natural life protected from the cunning vices of Satan.

Belt · The Truth
The first area is the waist, or that middle section of the body where the "muscles of the abdomen protect vital organs underneath, as well as provide structure for the spine, and help the body bend at the waist."[1] In other words, the muscles shield, they support and they facilitate movement. The muscles in the back also help with breathing by "raising and lowering the ribs."[1]

You are asked to "Gird your waist with the belt of truth" (Ephesians 6:14), that means the entire circumference of the mid section. A belt shields vulnerabilities and prevents undue exposure by effectively securing garments. Jesus said, "I am the way the truth and the life" (John 14:6). You need the all encompassing Truth wrapped around you continually. There must be nothing impeding progress as you advance into territories you acquire against the will of opposing forces. Krucik also provides a record of the organs being protected by Truth (Jesus), specifically,

> The intestines where digestion occurs; the liver (the body's largest organ) [sic] that filter toxins out of the body and aids in breaking food down before it passes to the digestive system; the stomach which stores the food; the pancreas which makes hormones and aids in the distribution of nutrients; the kidneys which process the blood the heart pumps before it circulates throughout the body; and the adrenal glands which secretes hormones that conserves sodium thus conserving water.[1]

Think about that for a minute. It is mind-blowing, and simply amazing. Consider all of the things God seeks to protect when He asks you to, "gird." Paul expresses confidence and certainty, saying, "I am confident of this very thing, that He who began a good work in you will perfect it until the day of Christ Jesus" (Philippians 1:6). You too have this assurance. God has not forsaken you.

It is important to keep the area shielded because the circumference of the waist indicates the body's risk of disease. One of the first places affected by unhealthy eating habits, or the body's response to sustained stress is the waistline. The body naturally produces excess cortisol (hydrocortisone) which settles there. "Cortisol is a powerful anti-inflammatory hormone that, in small quantities, speeds tissue repair, but in larger quantities depresses your body's immune defense system. A prolonged resistance reaction increases the risk of significant disease (including high blood pressure, diabetes and cancer);"[2] "Body cells function less effectively in this condition...As a result, your body becomes weak."[3] Also, cortisol controls mood, motivation and fear, a viral, instinctive emotion which was examined in detail in Chapter One. It is not an emotion that serves an anointed king well.

John 8:32 says, "You shall know the truth, and the truth

shall make you free." You will be free of fear and full of hope; free of sin and full of life; free to live according to God's precepts and to triumph continually. "When he, the Spirit of truth, comes, he will guide you into all the truth. He will not speak on his own; he will speak only what he hears, and he will tell you what is yet to come" (John 16:13). Truth safeguards you from the enemy. Don't leave home without it. You are also admonished to put on your breastplate of righteousness to ward off enemy attacks. At all costs, protect the heart.

Breastplate – The Heart
A breastplate is, "A piece of metal that covers a person's chest... it was part of the protective clothing (called armor) that soldiers wore in the past; a usually metal plate worn as defensive armor for the breast; a vestment worn in ancient times by a Jewish high priest and set with 12 gems bearing the names of the tribes of Israel." The breastplate was used in battle as well as in worship.

When God saw the spiritual state of His people, He spoke through the prophet Isaiah about Jesus Christ, saying, "His own arm achieved salvation for him, and his own righteousness sustained him. He put on righteousness as his breastplate, and the helmet of salvation on his head. He put on the garments of vengeance for clothing, and was clad with zeal as a cloak." (Isaiah 57:17). Jamee Rae states it well,

> The breastplate of righteousness is not something seen, but an attitude and a holy lifestyle that every Christian must personally enact...is necessary for defense during spiritual warfare...it is godliness, also known as the righteousness of God...following God's laws and His principles...and be willing to take off worldly layers and replace them with the good things of God. In doing so, the breastplate of righteousness will keep hearts pure and spirits alive.[4]

A breastplate protects by deflecting attacks from weapons that can cause fatalities. It covers the chest area, and extends downward and shields the heart. "The chest is the major hub for circulation. Not only is it where the heart lies, but it also houses major critical organs that require extensive amounts of blood flow to operate."[5]

Major airports which are considered hubs serve as central connection points for flight transfers. Without them, some travelers are stopped short of their final port. There are destinations they cannot reach without the hub. Hubs provide continuity, and increase a likelihood of successfully completed journeys. That is the heart's function as well and the end result is maximum functionality of the body, which is God's temple. The heart is a key facilitator in the accomplishment of His purpose.

You are fearfully and wonderfully made. God considered every eventuality when He created you in His image and His likeness. He designed your heart—simple in its complexity, complex in its simplicity—as a refueling tool which keeps the body filled with oxygen. Oxygen is "something that sustains, which facilitates combustions, yet does not burn. It is the most plentiful element on the earth." Oxygen purifies the air you breathe. It keeps the heart and other organs strong. As noted by Krucik, the heart:

> Provides blood throughout the entire circulatory system. Oxygenated blood is pumped from the heart to arteries, tissues and organs throughout the body; and deoxygenated blood flows back to the heart from organs and arteries. Without that blood flow from the heart; major organs would die. When the tissues all over the body, especially the brain, organs, and muscles, have used the oxygen, the blood returns to the heart through veins, such as the jugular veins in the neck and the auxiliary veins in the arms.[5]

Extended loss of oxygen causes brain damage and the body eventually dies. Oxygen is necessary for survival. You need it to live, to fight, to ignite a flame that keeps the cycle of life going. You need it for strength and sustenance. Therefore, the heart must be protected at all costs (Proverbs 4:23).

The breastplate of righteousness is designed to keep your heart secure so you can continue advancing into enemy territory to take it for Kingdom expansion. The breastplate also extends towards the waist area, providing double protection. Truth and righteousness prevail, in the best of times and in the worst of times. Having a protected heart is wonderful, yet your life cannot be fruitful unless your walk is right. Your feet must be properly safeguarded. Assured protection brings peace.

Feet – Your Walk

Damaged feet slow you down. They reduce or completely stop movement. You leave deformed footprints for those following. They may have been in a state of readiness, yet can no longer move quickly. They are now hindered by the formation of your fears and anxieties. Paul admonishes, it is necessary to have "Your feet fitted with the readiness that comes from the gospel of peace" (Ephesians 6:15). Without peace there is only heaviness, hesitation, and uncertainty.

Peace is power. It allows you to receive from the spiritual realm, unimpeded. A state of spiritual readiness is a byproduct. The prophet Isaiah says that, "The fruit of righteousness will be peace; its effect will be quietness and confidence forever" (Isaiah 32:17). It is no wonder God asks you to first secure yourself in truth, then protect your heart with righteousness. Peace creates the desire to move toward the things of God. It prepares you for the purposes of the Kingdom.

Peace is a balm that births boldness in a believer. An individual at rest is a ready conduit for *all* the work of the Lord. They pray and believe. They ask and receive, because they believe. There is a supernatural "knowing" that there is nothing too small or too great for God to accomplish through them. Someone in this spiritual state is unstoppable. No enemy territory is off limits to them. They are poised and ready to claim regions according to the Word of God. They believe it is theirs for the taking, under the power and authority of God. Because of this, miracles happen.

This is why Paul uses the word "fitted." A state of readiness should be molded to the shape of your feet, fixed, not easily removed or accidentally lost when in motion. According to James, "Peacemakers who sow in peace reap a harvest of righteousness" (James 3:18). There is that correlation again: peace and righteousness.

Kingdom warriors who hesitate at the wrong time will cause casualties not only to themselves but also to others. Put on the breastplate so there is nothing preventing you from moving when God directs. There is more armor you must wear to bolster both your offensive and defensive positions in battle. Next is a shield of faith.

Shield – Bold Faith

A heart full of faith keeps a spirit buoyant. Paul continues in his admonitions to correctly prepare for battle, saying, "In addition to all this, take up the shield of faith, with which you can extinguish all the flaming arrows of the evil one" (Ephesians 6:16). Faith repels doubt, faith castigates fear, and faith incites joy. Notice, Paul refers to faith as an extinguisher of the flames of the evil one's arrows. Put it on.

All sections of the armor are important. If you are wearing some and not others, there is unnecessary exposure. You may be girded with truth, and adorned in righteousness, but without faith sudden death can still occur. If faith is not operating in your life the enemy's flaming arrows can somehow find a way to your heart (Hebrews 11:6). You cannot extinguish the flaming arrows of the evil one without the power of God. How can you obtain the power if you do not believe (John 7:37-39)?

If you have faith, the battle is already won. It makes the enemy's weaponry ineffective, it also provides a calm assurance of victory (1 John 5:4). Faith is power.

Jesus said to His disciples, "Whoever believes in me will do the works I have been doing, and they will do even greater things than these" (John 14:14). It takes faith to activate the power. If you believe, there is no limit to what you can do for God. You are equipped to manifest the Kingdom in the earth.

There are other major areas that must be fortified. Protecting the body is important, but if the mind is exposed; you can still become a fatality. Your brain is a key organ which sustains life and must be safeguarded at all costs. It is a powerful tool in the hands of God or in the hands of Satan.

Helmet and Sword, Mind and Spirit

The brain is to the body what a CPU (Central Processing Unit) is to a computer. Without the CPU, there is no function. There is nothing to power it up, nothing to provide access, nothing to make it work. Paul also says, "Take the helmet of salvation and the sword of the Spirit, which is the word of God" (Ephesians 6:17). Salvation saves the soul, but the Word of God transforms it until it is a precision instrument. It is the Word that feeds, renews and changes your innermost being. It strengthens the Spirit man.

One precisely aimed bullet will kill the brain. No brain means no life. Individuals who are declared brain dead are removed from life support, because there is no longer hope they will ever live again. The brain sends communication throughout the entire body. It alerts you when there is danger. It initiates a fight or flight response. It tells the body when it needs to begin the healing process. If the brain is dead, it is only a matter of time before the entire body is also, unless the body is artificially sustained. Artificial sustenance does not help with brain function and the body is never able to move on its own again. [6] This is why prayer is so important in the arming process. It is supernatural protection.

The answers to the prayers of faith-filled believers cannot be hindered. They cannot be stopped by human intervention. While Rhoda and the rest of the Saints prayed for an imprisoned Peter, angels were in the cell shaking things up. They led him out of captivity, unharmed (Acts 12). The Bible instructs us to pray continually. It is the final piece of armor that holds everything together and works at maximum capacity.

Prayer – Your Fortified Spirit

Prayer topples giants and sends enemy soldiers fleeing in the night at the sound of their own footsteps (1 Samuel 17 & Judges 7). It causes wounded hearts to be healed and afflicted bodies to be made whole again. Paul asks that we "Pray in the Spirit on all occasions with all kinds of prayers and requests. With this in mind, be alert and always keep on praying for all the Lord's people" (Ephesians 6:18). Pray not just for yourself, but also for mankind. You are your brother's keeper. You have been asked to stand in the gap when necessary, to intercede for others just as Christ intercedes for you (Romans 8:34).

Prayer opens your spirit to deep revelations from God. In prayer Elisha asked God to open the eyes of his servant so he could see beyond the natural. His fears disappeared when spiritual reinforcements were revealed (2 Kings 6:17). Prayer had Elijah so connected to God, he supernaturally heard the sound of rain falling before there were any natural signs of its coming (1 Kings 18:41-45). Prayer revealed things to Daniel that no other human being understood. The revelation God downloaded into his spirit could only be interpreted by him (Daniel 2).

Prayer is a gate that unlocks the heavens. It draws the light of God. It illuminates every corner until darkness is completely dispelled. It activates an open heaven and blocks the move of the enemy. He cannot prevail against Saints of God who know how to pray and understand the power they wield.

You are the light of the world, but Satan lives in darkness. "What communion hath light with darkness?" (2 Corinthians 6:14). Light exposes what darkness conceals. It reveals the works of the enemy. There is a slim chance that you can hit a target in the dark, but your words of prayer are pointed arrows that hit and expose hidden enemies every single time. God shows you battle front strategy to understand the enemy. You will know how he works and how to defeat him.

The battlefront is the area of major confrontation between the forces of darkness and angels of light. An anointed vessel commands action and counteraction on the battlefront.

THE BATTLEFRONT

When the anointing comes from God, there is nothing anyone can do to stop it. They can try – but it will not work. God used a Persian King (Cyrus) to do great things for His people (2 Chronicles 36:22). Cyrus was anointed to function on God's behalf. He championed the cause of a God he did not believe in; a God he did not serve. He was handpicked to fight for the people of Israel.

At God's direction, King Cyrus returned all of the items King Nebuchadnezzar had taken from the Temple in Jerusalem. God used him to restore what rightfully belonged in the place of worship, and make a declaration, a decree, on behalf of the mission. Who dared challenge it? (2 Chronicles 36:23).

God also ensured King Cyrus had the resources needed to complete the task. First, He anointed and called him, then He bestowed a title of honor upon him. He strengthened Cyrus, brought prosperity, rained down righteousness and caused it to grow. He made sure the path of the mission was cleared and gave him favor with other kings. Cyrus knew that he did not draw the blessing. It was God orchestrating it for His people's sake (Isaiah 45).

King Cyrus gained successes with God's blessing, as God took hold of his right hand and subdued nations before him, leveled mountains, broke down gates of bronze, and cut through bars of iron. He gave him the treasures of darkness and riches stored in secret places. He put power in his voice as he decreed. It was all about bringing God's mandated mission for Israel to pass (Isaiah 45). That particular battle had no great opposition, but battles are not usually unopposed.

Strategic Warfare

Gideon, like Cyrus, was also chosen, called and anointed. He did not know his power, but God sent him into battle. He had no self respect, and thought he had little or no respect among his people. He saw himself as insignificant and potentially ineffective. He could not have been more wrong. His anointing was different. It enhanced a spiritual download. The help he received from God caused him to win swiftly, with almost no effort. Here are some significant points about the steps Gideon took:-

1. First he prayed; asking for strategy (Judges 6:15).
2. He brought his insecurities into the open. "My clan is the weakest in Manasseh, and I am the least in my family" (Judges 6:15).

3. He worshipped (Judges 6:18, 24). After Gideon worshipped God immediately began downloading strategies to him.
4. He made sure that he and his family were unified in worship by removing idols and building an altar to God. Concerns about their spiritual state would not be a distraction for Gideon (Judges 6:27-31).
5. He embraced the mission. Gideon issued a call to battle and to arms. He found his strength and rose to purpose (Judges 6:34).
6. He continued to develop his relationship with God. There was still some uncertainty about whether they would win the battle and Gideon had a real conversation with God about his trepidation (Judges 6:36-39).
7. God told him how to shape his battalion and gave instructions regarding who would be great soldiers (Judges 7:2-7).
8. Gideon obeyed (Judges 7:8).
9. God sent him on a reconnaissance mission and he followed instructions (Judges 7:10-14).
10. After he gathered intelligence information, he worshipped (Judges 7:15).
11. He encouraged his army, imparting the confidence he had to them (Judges 7:15-16).
12. He equipped his men (Judges 7:16).
13. He led them into battle (Judges 7:17-18).
14. He took territory and necessary resources (Judges 7:24-25).
15. He conquered (Judges 7:25).
16. He gained wisdom (Judges 8:1-3).
17. He became a true warrior, actively seeking conquest and taking territories (Judges 8:4-21).
18. Israel asked him to rule (Judges 8:22).
19. He brought forty years of peace to the land (Judges 8:28).

The kingly anointing is not restricted to an office. It is bestowed as God sees fit. Gideon, who initially saw himself as lowly and incapable, became a warrior, a conqueror and a ruler.

He may not have been a king, but he functioned as one. He rose into the kingly anointing and had great successes. He had not seen himself governing, but God knew. Consequently, so did all of Israel. Gideon conquered and subdued armies because of the anointing and through the power of God. The power to subdue is only present if the power of God is on the inside.

You too can have that power, but it only makes you a habitation when you rightly connect and establish relationship with God. The fruit of the relationship is heavy duty weaponry against the enemy. There is nothing preventing you from firmly planting your feet in territory and watching them scurry away resignedly.

THE POWER TO SUBDUE

Advancing on a spiritual enemy with natural weapons is spiritual suicide. The first major requirement is a relationship with God. The second, is to gird yourself with the armor of God in order to prevail. The enemy will not be able to withstand you if you are properly armed. You can deflect his attacks while advancing into territory he has taken, and reclaim it. Then, you need to sound the battle cry in prayer (Ephesians 6:18). When you have received inspiration and instruction from your General (God, your ultimate warrior), armed yourself and sounded the battle cry, only then can you can step out in full power to subdue. Do not be afraid, you have already won.

You cannot launch a successful offensive from a position of fear. If you were asked to destroy weapons as an enemy advanced on you, it would be difficult to not become fearful. Massive doses of courage would be in order. In Ezekiel thirty-nine God told Ezekiel to prophesy to the people of Israel that for seven years they were to use their weapons as fuel—the shields, bows and arrows, clubs and spears (vs. 9-10). During that time, they had victories but not with natural weapons. They obeyed and God did the work. Their enemies were annihilated. They had to trust God completely. Using spiritual weapons as fuel caused them to gain power, strength and a season of continual victory.

Burning your weapons means surrendering them to the Holy Spirit. Submit them to His power, and trust that His glory will manifest as He moves on your behalf. The weapons of your warfare are mighty, but the fire of the Holy Spirit is mightier. Put your faith on fire. Allow a concentrated prayer life to create rapid movement and intense heat in the realm of the spirit. Become consumed by truth and God's embracing redemption. Let the Word burn in your heart as the flames of righteousness illuminate your life. His light will shine through you.

Only a prepared vessel can become a chosen vessel. It is impossible to gain the power to subdue if you are unwilling to surrender to God's will. Only through total surrender do you submit yourself to the necessary changes in your transformational process. God will never give you more than you can handle. Every component in your development is a building block that has a specific place in the final form of your spirit.

You must know how to be under authority in order to gain authority. Adam and Eve were under God's authority when He gave them dominion. Only when they moved from under that authority and obeyed another did they lose position in the realm of the spirit (Genesis 3). Elisha served under Elijah until he received a double portion. He moved in power and authority, accomplishing similar and greater things than Elijah had accomplished. You must be able to handle the power that comes with authority. Do not become prideful.

Power intoxicates if you are not properly prepared for it. Intoxication incapacitates you and eradicates the ability to govern, subdue or have real dominion. When someone with dominion annihilates their enemy, there is a posture which identifies them as a true warrior and conqueror.

A novice becomes puffed up, because winning is not the norm. They lose focus on further missions because they are too busy looking around to see who noticed they won a victory. Everything is about them, and it is easy for them to take their eyes off of the one who gave them power. They begin to focus solely on themselves.

You must know how to handle power. Some gain authority only to abuse it. Saul is a great example. He allowed power to change him in a way that was not pleasing to God. He became prideful, then vengeful (although there was nothing to avenge). His focus was single minded. He got completely off course and was no longer driven by purpose, but by his own fleshly desires. It was a costly error.

You must act like a champion, but do so under the anointing of the Holy Spirit. Never lose sight of the fact that He is the one who makes your champion status possible (Romans 8:37). Power drapes the soul of the conqueror, but should not control him or her.

CONQUEROR'S POWER

When King David slaughtered the Amalekites at Ziklag he did not laud the win over his subjects. He was gracious. Two hundred men had been too tired to follow him into battle, but rather than keeping a portion of the spoils from them as some of the men who had fought suggested, David included them in the distribution (1 Samuel 30:23-31).

David's stance taught his warriors lessons about the carriage and bearing of a true conqueror. It displayed his character and influence, and was a demonstration of how conqueror's power should sit on the shoulders of one to whom power is a norm rather than an occasional event. David understood that God was the source of his success. He recognized the need to continue to honor God in the choices he made, and exhibited the following principles:

1. A true conqueror never loses sight of the needs of the men and women who serve him, no matter how menial their tasks may be.
2. A true conqueror knows how to make even the smallest in the group feel like a valued member of his army.

3. A true conqueror is generous. He does not keep all of the rewards to himself.
4. A true conqueror understands how to foster mutual respect among the ranks.
5. A true conqueror establishes positive solutions as a part of the battalion's lifestyle.
6. A true conqueror increases his army by displaying kindness to his communities and surrounding areas.
7. A true conqueror never forgets those whose lives he has touched, or those who have touched his.
8. A true conqueror is listened to, observed and obeyed by those serving him.

Not all who dominate are true conquerors. An individual who properly handles conqueror's power knows how to maintain a level head and humble heart when they are being lauded with praise and accolades. God trusts this person with dominion, because they do not rule with a spirit that is drunk on the power of influence.

DOMINION

Joseph was sold and imprisoned before he actually gained dominion. As a slave he ruled in his master's house. As a prisoner he had the jailer's keys to the prison. He did not seem like a probable candidate to rule, but he had spiritual dominion. It caused him to stand out as a leader, even in adverse times.

Daniel also walked in dominion. Though he was in captivity for most of his life, his prayer life, strong faith, humility, spirit of excellence and spirit of sacrifice caused him to carry an anointing which compelled kings and subdued enemies. His actions and heart attitude exuded authority.

Religion has no dominion. It does not matter how often you pray or read the Bible, you will not have dominion with a bad attitude, or if you are treating others poorly. Do not expect dominion to be bestowed upon you if you have a prideful spirit or a vengeful heart. Be humble, forgiving, loving, compassionate, courageous and faithful.

When you become a dwelling place for the spirit of God, dominion attaches itself to your spirit. You govern in the realm of the spirit and rule in the earth. Moses had great dominion because he walked so closely with God. This measure of dominion allows you to experience God's manifest presence. It draws the glory every time.

THE GLORY

To draw God's glory you must know how to receive glorification without becoming contaminated. The anointing not only draws the glory of God; it also brings glorification from individuals, people who are well meaning. In Second Chronicles twenty-six, King Uzziah accomplished great things, and "his fame spread far and wide, for he was greatly helped until he became powerful. But after Uzziah became powerful, his pride led to his downfall" (vs. 15-16).

He stepped out of his purpose and into another's when he attempted to do the work of the Priests. He would not listen to those who tried to stop him, and God struck Uzziah with leprosy because he defiled the Temple.

Contaminated kings do not handle glory well. It is a sad thing to become so blinded and deafened by pride that you are no longer concerned about whether or not God is pleased with your actions. King Nebuchadnezzar was given lofty positions and power, "But when his heart became arrogant and hardened with pride, he was deposed from his royal throne and stripped of his glory" (Daniel 5:20). If your heart is contaminated, it will block God's glory.

King Uzziah became a blocking spirit, and it was only after his death that Isaiah saw the glory of the Lord manifest (Isaiah 59:1-3). "In the Old Testament, the most common word for *glory* is the Hebrew *kabod*, meaning "heavy in weight." When you glorify someone, you recognize his importance, or the "weight," of some desirable uniqueness he possesses. Beauty, majesty, and splendor are the main ideas the word seeks to convey."[7] God says, "You will seek me and find me when you seek me with all your heart" (Jeremiah 29:13). If you seek with all your heart, you safeguard it against the things that hinder you from experiencing God's fullness. Avoid becoming someone who blocks the revelation of God's glory. Guard your heart from the sin of pride.

The glory is reserved for the anointed, those with a life that will stand in the purity and the intensity of God's presence. In the New Testament, the Greek word for glory is *doxazo*, and its usage is meant to convey a sense of brilliance, or radiance. [7] Jesus Christ experienced the glory of His Father's presence in its fullness. He, Himself, became the glory and radiated the presence and nature of God (Hebrews 1:3-4).

Just as the moon reflects the light of the sun, you can reflect the light of Christ. There are hindrances which seek to keep you unfocused and distracted, but you must keep pressing. The Bible says, "Iniquities separate you from your God; and sins cause Him to hide his face from you" (Isaiah 59:2). Continually seek His truth. Be driven to diligently study the Bible, and live a lifestyle of worship.

The glory is accessible to you, but you must do what is required to access it. The Bible says, "The Lord rises upon you and his glory appears over you. Nations will come to your light, and Kings to the brightness of your dawn," (Isaiah 60:2-3). The entire chapter tells of the wonderful things to come *after* the glory manifests. It was a prophetic word from Isaiah and is relevant even now.

A pure kingly anointing always draws God's Glory. It is time to rise in stature, assume a position of readiness and take what is rightfully yours as a child of God. You are a part of the Kingdom government.

A king rules for life. Throughout history many kings did not die of old age. Instead they lost their lives in battle, usually a battle for territory. It was kill or be killed. The same principle applies to the spiritual battle in which many are now engaged. It is important to fight with the right weapons. Fight to win! Fight to advance, to gain and rule. The enemy seeks to conquer but his weapons are inferior. Rise king, dominion is yours. God has given you the land. Take it.

⊹

Prayer

Dear Heavenly Father, I know that now is the time to govern under Your anointing. I am ready to become accurately armed. I will remain humble and treat my fellow warriors with the respect that is due to them as we annihilate the enemy together and take territory in your name.

I will walk in your way and study to gain a deeper understanding of Kingdom tactics. I am relying on You for the impartation of revolutionary strategies and will obey as you command. I yield myself completely. Use me as You will, for Your glory. In Jesus' name, Amen.

Chapter Six

THE PROPHETIC ANOINTING

The prophetic word either comes through someone in the prophetic office or through someone with the prophetic gift. The responsibility of this call is great and the weight of the gift should not be casually observed. In Bible days the prophetic word was often given to a king or to the subjects of a kingdom. It served as a formidable weapon in an anointed king's arsenal. It heralded good news or issued proclamations of judgment against contaminated kings. Only those who believed saw the value of the prophetic word and understood it was sincere and necessary.

The prophetic word is powerful. It pierces, compels, directs, warns, relays, comforts, and shows mercy. The bearers of the prophetic word continually live under the weight of its responsibility. Jeremiah wept and was often jailed because of the revelatory word he carried.

In Zechariah chapters one and two God admonishes His people to learn from the mistakes of their ancestors. He expresses a desire to bless. He speaks through Zechariah saying, "Return to Jerusalem with mercy, and there my house will be rebuilt. And the measuring line will be stretched out over Jerusalem,' declares the LORD Almighty. 'Proclaim further: This is what the LORD Almighty says: 'My towns will again overflow with prosperity, and the LORD will again comfort Zion and choose Jerusalem" (vs. 16-17). Words such as these are easier to deliver and are often better received.

The prophetic word comes without consideration of the messenger's ease or difficulty in handling the assignment. It circumvents or supersedes plans or efforts conceived in the flesh. Prophets speak what thus saith the Lord, avoiding contaminants which dilute and pollute the anointing. They suffer dire consequences when they utter lies or partial proclamations in compromise.

A prophetic word will not be stopped. Even if the prophet is disobedient (not relaying the message as it is received) or if the people disbelieve, the prophetic word will come to pass. It is all encompassing in its purpose. Like an avalanche beginning at the top of a high mountain—it does not reverse course. Instead it gains momentum as it gets closer to manifestation (Zechariah 1:6).

Prophets are carefully selected by God. Not everyone can handle the power of the prophetic call or shoulder the tremendous responsibility it brings. An individual in this office must be able to tolerate whatever comes. Sometimes prophets suffer for the truth they deliver, or they are appreciated because of it. Only God's clear and accurate message will successfully guide His people through turbulent times. It is desperately needed today.

The prophetic anointing was vital in olden days. Prophets were beaten, thrown in prison, ridiculed and scorned. Like Jeremiah, they may have felt like giving up, or they may have been deathly afraid. Nonetheless, the gift was theirs. They carried the mantle like a badge of honor, understanding the strength it required and the price they must pay.

No one should take the prophetic call lightly, least of all those who have been blessed with it. God speaks directly to them (Deuteronomy 18:18). Those who speak falsely in His name will pay a dreadful price (Deuteronomy 18:20).

Some try to pervert the prophetic gift. The Bible warns about them. Modern day deceptions are uttered for financial gain, and false prophets manipulate unsuspecting people into supporting and propagating their quasi-ministry. God refers to them as ravening wolves in sheep's clothing (Matthew 7:15). He also challenges man to test spirits to ensure they are not receiving false prophecies (1 John 1:4). Some will be so convincing, people will be deceived (Matthew 24:24). Only prophecies spoken by those called and chosen will bear God's truth.

THE CALL

The prophetic call is a daily cross. Samuel was chosen long before he was born. His mother, Hannah, could not bear children because "God had shut up her womb" (I Samuel 1:5, KJV). God allowed her husband's second wife (Peninnah) who had many children to repeatedly taunt Hannah about her state of barrenness. *Peninnah was necessary.* What she had to offer was not good, but it heightened Hannah's desperation. It motivated her to vow that if God allowed her to have a son, she would offer him back unto Him all the days of his life.

Her distress brought her to the attention of Eli, the priest, who prayed with her and decreed, "The God of Israel would grant what she asked of him" (1 Samuel 1:17). After the decree, "Hannah worshipped; and God remembered her. He opened her womb and she conceived and bare a son, and called his name Samuel, saying, Because I have asked him of the Lord" (1 Samuel 1:20). Hannah's closed womb produced desperation which compelled prayer and worship. It sent her to the Temple and drove her to her knees. She encountered someone there with a word which brought peace. Peace caused her to stop worrying. When she stopped worrying, the answer to her prayer manifested (1 Samuel 1:1-20).

Adversity is a necessary component. You petition God for things—position, authority—but will you pay the price to have them? Can you handle the process to the promise? Sometimes, unless adversity steers you in the right direction, you set out on a course that is not designed for you. God is sovereign. He knows what you need to draw heaven.

Adversity is like a spiritual stop light. You may be called, chosen and anointed, but without the process there is likely some anomaly the devil can put his hands on and use it to contaminate your anointing. Adversity will direct you toward destiny. Hannah's vow put Samuel in the Temple under Eli's wing where he was taught to listen for and identify the voice of God. It made him a powerful and accurate prophet in Israel (1 Samuel 3:19).

You are never alone in the midst of adversity. God provides an anchor to ground you in the process. Remember what He said to Jeremiah? "Before I formed you in the womb I knew you, before you were born I set you apart; I appointed you as a prophet to the nations" (Jeremiah 1:5). He is ever present and able to sustain you. You must keep your eyes on Him. Submit to those in authority over you, to be trained and equipped for your calling. There are things they must impart. This is only possible if you humbly receive and appropriate their teachings.

Anointed prophets challenge those they are training to carry the Mantle. When Elisha expressed a hunger for impartation of a double portion of Elijah's anointing, Elijah challenged him to maintain focus (2 Kings 2:9-10). It kept him in a state of readiness. I can see Elisha carrying out his daily tasks, with eyes glued to Elijah. His pace quickens and he is at Elijah's side in a split second. It made his spirit sensitive; his senses sharpened. Elisha watches for so long and for so hard that he mirrors Elijah's movements. He is intricately locked on to the man he has been serving diligently. I believe he became adept at jumping over obstacles in his path. He probably had quite a few false starts, prematurely rushing to Elijah's side because he did not want to miss the event that would initiate his move toward destiny.

Legacy bearers are not attention seekers. They are not looking to be showcased. Although Elisha wanted a double portion of the anointing; it was only because he admired the stature and the gift of the man he served. He likely prayed, "Lord I want to honor you and the life of the man I serve by being more than just a good servant. I want to be a great man of God like Elijah so it will be known how much I appreciate his teachings."

His desire was to spend as much time as he could with Elijah and gain the fullness of the legacy through service. He understood the inevitability of Elijah's departure, yet it pained his heart when he actually left. Elisha mourned (2 Kings 2:12). He was grieving because he loved Elijah. He did not mourn for long though, there was work to be done. What followed was an almost instantaneous manifestation of the double anointing on Elisha's life.

The level of relationship produces the fruit of the anointing. In order for a prophet's anointing to be consistently accurate, they need a strong relationship with the Lord. It keeps the spirit completely open for revelation. Also necessary is accurate connection to a mentor. Elisha carried serious power after the chariot ascended. The potency of his anointing is clearly seen after Elijah is taken up in a chariot of fire.

Elisha parts the Jordan River by striking it with a cloak (2 Kings 2). He advised kings. He commanded the elements and they obeyed. He rose into the anointing and was a force for the work of God. You have to be prepared for all that comes with the prophetic anointing; both the adulation and the criticism.

THE THORN

Anointed prophets are required to rise above the "thorn" in their flesh. A prophet under attack may experience an increase in their anointing because the attack prompts a greater dependence on God, amplifying the power. They do not seek to bend the will of individuals. The power of the oil causes people to yield to the spirit of God.

Ahaziah had no real power over Elijah, yet he was a thorn in his flesh (2 Kings 1). Although he knew Elijah accurately prophesied his parent's death, it was inconceivable to repent, it was as if he believed more in his own power than in the power of God. He did not consider that God's power (demonstrated by a pure, anointed prophet) commands respect and reverence. Eventually, people come to honor the gift, the function and the anointing.

A legacy of evil produces death. Ahaziah continued his father's legacy of evil. Shortly after he began ruling, he fell and injured himself. Instead of seeking God, he sought counsel from Baal-Zebub, a false god. He wanted to know whether or not he would recover from the injury.

While he was consulting a false god, the Lord sent an angel with a prophetic message for Ahaziah, asking, "Is it because there is no God in Israel that you are sending messengers to consult Baal-Zebub, the god of Ekron? Therefore you will not leave the bed you are lying on. You will certainly die!" (2 Kings 1:6). The prophesy came to pass. Clear spiritual sight is a prophet's protection. It produces an accurate word.

CLEAR VISION

An accurate prophetic word is like an arrow that has already left the bow and is in en route to the target. It cannot be recalled. It does not stop once in motion.

Nothing hinders the fulfillment of the prophetic word. King Ahab could not escape the prophecy of his death. He disguised himself in battle and the word still found him. In the heat of the fight, "a random bow hit him between the sections of his armor and killed him" (1 Kings 22:34).

Joseph's prophetic dream did not die when his brothers threw him into a pit and sold him into slavery. It did not die when he was sent to prison. The word lived and breathed life into him until it came to fruition. The same is true for every prophesy spoken of Jesus. He came, He suffered, and He died and rose again.

Anointed prophets support the Kingly anointing by presenting a word that equips them for war. It often includes battle strategy. The Bible says, "Surely the Sovereign LORD does nothing without revealing his plan to his servants the prophets. The lion has roared— who will not fear? The Sovereign LORD has spoken—who can but prophesy?" (Amos 3:7-8). The prophetic word guided King Jehoshaphat when Moab and Ammon came against him. God used it to provide strategy and to reassure the king that there would be victory (2 Chronicles 20:14-17).

Anointed prophets bring words of judgment to errant kings. King Jehoshaphat's son, Jehoram who ascended to the throne after his father's death, did evil, and God sent Elijah to issue the consequences of his actions through an accurate prophetic word (2 Chronicles 21:12-15). The words of the prophet came to pass, and King Jehoram died in shame, because the contamination from Ahab had made its way down to him. Not only were his ways perverted, he led the people of his Kingdom into perversion as well. His manner of death brought dishonor, and the people disassociated themselves from him at the time of his passing. Although he "was buried in the City of David, [they did not place him] in the tombs of the kings" (2 Chronicles 21:20). Not even the burial site was good enough for him. It was for those who served with honor.

The anointing strengthens the prophet. They do not change course because of intimidation. They reiterate the authentic Word of God, understanding it may not always be well received. The Prophet Micaiah who prophesied King Ahab's death, went to the court when Ahab called, and spoke knowing Ahab would be hard pressed to believe what God said. He spoke the word, was questioned, spoke it again providing more details, was chided, slapped and eventually sent to prison (1 Kings 22). Anointed prophets proclaim the truth, barring consequence.

Anointed prophets walk in the power of God and the fullness of His grace. God's grace covers His true prophets. Moses had an opportunity to see that grace at work in his life when his brother Aaron and sister Miriam spoke against him secretly. God called them all together and said,

> Listen to my words: "When there is a prophet among you, I, the LORD, reveal myself to them in visions, I speak to them in dreams. But this is not true of my servant Moses; he is faithful in all my house. With him I speak face to

face, clearly and not in riddles; he sees the form of the LORD. Why then were you not afraid to speak against my servant Moses? (Numbers 12:6-8).

It was clear that God had Moses' back, and would deal with anyone coming against him, no matter the affiliation. The knowledge of this support allows prophets to freely and openly deliver all messages without compromise.

Anointed prophets protect the king's anointing. An anointed prophet's weapons storehouse is continuously armed when it is equipped with a pure heart and an accurate word. When the prophet Nathan learned that Adonijah was trying to seize David's throne from Solomon, he immediately alerted Bathsheba (Solomon's mother) so she could intercede on behalf of her son. He did so because of his love and profound respect for King David. He was aware that David expected Solomon to succeed him. If Nathan had not done what was required to protect the throne, it would have taken much longer for the Lord's Tabernacle to be built (1 Kings 1).

Three anointings came together to protect the throne and advance the purpose of God in both David's and Solomon's lives. Prophet, priest and king (Nathan, Zadok and David) worked to ensure Solomon was successfully crowned. The priest poured the oil from the horn to anoint Solomon for the throne (1 Kings 1:10-14), and collectively, they paved the way for him to execute divine assignments that were essential for Israel's advancement. He built God's house, a place of worship, and established a season of peace, because of his anointing.

Anointed prophets leave a powerful legacy. There is no greater example of triumphant succession than the disciples who served Christ. They were left to carry the gospel of the Kingdom to the nations of the world. In Acts two, they united anointings and magnified the power which had been endowed by the Holy Spirit. Thousands came to Christ because of an effective and powerful legacy, and they went on to function mightily in their ministry gifts.

Another strong example is seen in Second Kings chapter two. Elijah left a powerful legacy to Elisha. Through service, submission, and humility, Elisha was literally adorned in the spirit of the leader under whose tutelage his character and courage was birthed. What also developed was an uncompromising will to serve priests and kings as Elijah had done before. He wanted to be accurate and effective with the power received through the double anointing.

Anointed prophets understand the work must continue when they are gone. This knowledge initiates training and teaching that allows the protégé to step into the role with no breach. It is easy to do so because the driving force is to fulfill purpose and position those coming behind to continue leading the charge. Only prophets who are called, chosen and anointed will impart God designed methods to accomplish the mission.

Beware of false prophets. Those who prophesy out of their imagination follow their own spirit. They have no revelation. God commanded the prophet Ezekiel to prophesy against them. He spoke to ones misleading the people, warning of judgment and punishment for prophets speaking lies. They kept the hearts of the nation turned away from God and encouraged the people to remain in their evil ways (Ezekiel 13). God's wrath is reserved for them.

Prophets are God's delegates. It is dangerous to offer prophetic words when you have not been called or anointed to do so (Jeremiah 23:10-12). The power is in the anointing. It protects the function, the office and the people. It is foolish to try to function without it.

The disciples operated in that power on the day of Pentecost. It spread like wild fire then, and continues to gain force every day. You are made to carry the fire. Not to contain it, but allow it to touch people wherever you go. God has given you power to impact nations.

FIRE IN MY BONES

An anointed prophet has a burning resolve to endure and persevere so the unadulterated prophetic word is spoken as

God commands. Their attitude is, "not my will but yours Lord." They may become disheartened, and sometimes feel challenged to handle the responsibility of the call, however, the Word drives them to release it as it is spoken to their spirit.

The fire in purpose drives you to the Cross for rejuvenation and strength. It helps you to maintain purity so the messages from God are undiluted. When Jeremiah was beaten and jailed, he found himself in a desperately desolate place. He questioned the authenticity of God's Word and cursed the day he was born. But, no matter how much he tried, he could not contain what he had been anointed to speak. Jeremiah's transparency demonstrated the depth of his despair and resolve. In the midst of his groaning, he said, "The word of the LORD has brought me insult and reproach all day long. But if I say, "I will not mention his word or speak anymore in his name," his word is in my heart like a fire, a fire shut up in my bones. I am weary of holding it in; indeed, I cannot" (Jeremiah 20:8-9).

Fire is hot and it moves quickly. It consumes or purifies everything in its path. If you are unable to elude it, there is no escaping. It will course through every vein, muscle, tissue and organ of your body until all you are is fire. The fire of the Holy Spirit gripped Jeremiah and there was no letting go. He was never forced, but he understood and accepted his purpose. It was enough to give him strength to rise up time and time again to function in his calling. This type of fire positions you to hear and see the mysteries of Heaven.

THE MYSTERIES OF HEAVEN

There is a realm of divine revelation that is only open to the prophet. God communicates it to their spirit. Daniel had an accurate prophetic anointing. There were things God revealed then asked him not to speak of them. He kept them to himself, and when the time was right they were released. Some of these prophecies are chronicled in Daniel chapters eleven and twelve.

There are prophesies that are for a specific time only. Daniel was instructed to record his revelations on scrolls. The documented prophesies would be relevant in the future. It is the mission of those living in a time of prophetic fulfillment to interpret and share those revelations. Daniel was instructed not to speak, and he obeyed. Now we see many of those prophetic words unfolding before our eyes.

John was also charged with powerful revelations of things to come. What he saw would have been difficult for many to understand at the time. They were detailed and intricately woven into his spirit. He also received instructions to write the visions on scrolls because the mysteries revealed were for times to come (Revelations 1:17-19). John never experienced them in his lifetime, and many things still have not manifested to this day (Revelations 1:9-11).

Every anointed prophet hears from God, but there are certain mysteries only revealed to some. They are shared with the ones who have an exceptional kind of fortitude and resolve, individuals for whom the responsibility is a weight they are willing and able to bear. God can trust them implicitly with the knowledge of hard things, and He can rely on them to do exactly as He asks. Imagine being the bearer of some of the prophetic words written in the Bible; or the seer of supernatural revelations. The things John saw were surreal even to him, but he obeyed. Because of that, today we have a road map of things to come.

The call to the prophetic is sacred. The prophet Isaiah said, "The Spirit of the Sovereign LORD is on me, because the LORD has anointed me" (Isaiah 61:1). In Luke 4:18, Jesus read this same statement, then stated, "Today this scripture is fulfilled in your hearing" (Luke 4:21). Isaiah had spoken and recorded truth. Jesus brought it to life and validated it.

Prophets have no realistic expectation of immediate validation of the words they speak. God authenticates the prophecy in time. This is why accuracy is tantamount. The prophet is never accurate unless he is correctly plugged into the spirit of The Living God. It is the Spirit that sustains his life.

The prophetic word is not for the prophet, it is for the people. Whether the word brings life, judgment, correction, or direction, it is for the people. If you have been called to this office, do not take the responsibility lightly. Remain close to God. Speak with Him often (that means speaking, waiting and listening). Consult Him regarding not only that which He wishes you to speak, but also when you should speak (John 16:13). Someone's life may depend upon it. Trust God with your gift and your call.

Resolve to declare prophecies from God. Be assured that He is with you always. He is doing a new thing, just like in the days of Isaiah (Isaiah 43:19). Say like David, God alone is your portion and you will not be shaken (Psalm 16). You will not die, but live to proclaim all that the Lord has spoken to you (Psalm 118:17).

Prayer

Dear Heavenly Father, please help me to not feel weighted down by the call, but to be humbled by it; ready always to receive from You. Help me to press into You as I handle any persecution that may come. Allow me to clearly see all that you reveal. Cause the fire of your Holy Spirit to burn in me. Consume me, compel me, guide me as I live on purpose and as purpose drives me to function as a Kingdom warrior.

Daddy God, I know that the path may not always be easy, but I trust you. Prepare me for all that is to come. In Jesus' name, Amen.

Chapter Seven

❧

THE PRIESTLY ANOINTING

Priests have the ability, the authority and the strategy to break through every barrier the enemy devises. You are a "living stone...being built into a spiritual house to be a holy priesthood, offering spiritual sacrifices acceptable to God through Jesus Christ" (1 Peter 2:5). Meditate on that for just a moment.

Stones are hard, yet useful. They can break glass, shatter wood, and create friction when they come in contact with other stones. Purposefully piled stones become steps for someone trying to get out of a ditch. They can be used to fashion a bridge or block a pathway. They are also used to build structures, in this case spiritual houses.

A contaminated priest cannot build a pure spiritual house. As a result they become useless stones which cause others to stumble. Peter said, "We are royal Priests, called to declare the praises of Him who called us out into his marvelous light" (1 Peter 2:9). This declaration of praise is designed to exalt our King and draw others to Him. An impure priest offers praise that does not encourage anyone to seek God. They hinder the process of their own spiritual maturity.

To successfully present Christ's nature, there are steps a future priest must take to be prepared. First, the foundation of the spiritual house starts with a thorough cleansing (1 Peter 2:1). It is for the ones who take the call to priesthood seriously. They understand the necessity of purity to secure the potency of the anointing. Second, the priest requires a level of maturity to carry the power. Peter provides insight here as well, advising, "Like newborn babies, crave pure spiritual milk, so that by it you may grow up in your salvation" (1 Peter 2:2). These are steps that properly position you to be anointed as a priest.

Purification: From Head to Toe

Priests must go through the qualification process. Beyond the call is the process to righteousness; the conduit to true spiritual power. Beyond the call is the path to purification and preparation. Vessels of silver and gold are made pure in the fire. Although pure, they still require regular cleaning, and polishing to remain beautiful. How else will they be fully prepared, not only for the work, but to take on all opposition to the work?

It is important that no one steps into the priestly assignment without proper development. You must endure accurate preparation so there is no undue exposure to destruction. Aaron and his sons were called as priests, but they had to undergo several levels of purification before they were fully qualified to go before God on behalf of the people.

- They were called by God (Leviticus 8:1-3).
- They were cleansed (Leviticus 8:6).
- They were properly adorned and identified as priests (Leviticus 8:7).
- Their hearts were protected (Leviticus 8:8).
- Their minds were shielded (Leviticus 8: 9).
- The place where they would serve was anointed, and they were anointed (Leviticus 8:10-12).
- The priests serving with Aaron were also properly adorned and covered (Leviticus 8:13).
- They were consecrated (Leviticus 8:14). The process required a sacrifice, and they had to touch the sacrifice in order to become fully consecrated. They could not stand afar off.
- Their worship was purified (Leviticus 8:15).

Anything blocking the process of complete consecration was offered up. Internal organs are not visible to the naked eye. It is easy for them to unknowingly become shrouded by excess, malformation and disease. Only upon extensive examination (usually with equipment with the ability to "see" beyond flesh) are they discovered. Only by cutting away flesh can they be removed. Only by fire can they be immediately and utterly destroyed (Leviticus 8:16).

Overcome anxiety about flaws and weaknesses so they do no become a hindrance. You must be able to remain at the door of the Tabernacle, entrenched in the task God has called you to. Flaws and insecurities become impediments to the function if they are not placed under the blood. See them and accept that they exist. God has the power to help you to overcome.

The anointing costs a life. Flesh was handled at the door of the Tabernacle. It was not brought inside. You may want to bring flesh with you, but it must be utterly destroyed for God to use you. Whatever remains has to be burned completely (Leviticus 8:17).

Many want to coast through to purpose and destiny effortlessly, but the ultimate offering unto God is birthed in fire. Your offering should not be corrupted by any residue. Go through the purification process until you become the ultimate weapon against the enemy.

Contaminants in a priest's life abort destiny. Eli's sons (Hophni and Phinehas) defiled the Temple by repeatedly "treating the Lord's offering with contempt" (1 Samuel 2:17) and "[Sleeping] with the women who served at the entrance" (1 Samuel 2:22). Eli knew about their infractions, and questioned them about wrong doing; but he never held them accountable. He did not correct them, so they served no godly purpose in the Temple.

The consequence for not only their dishonor, but also Eli's since he had not removed them from the Temple, was swift and final. The prophetic word was sharp and uncompromising. God said, "Far be it from Me; for those who honor Me I will honor, and those who despise Me shall be lightly esteemed. Behold, the days are coming that I will cut off your arm and the arm of your father's house, so that there will not be an old man in your house" (1 Samuel 2:30-31). It was a warning they ignored.

Allowing his sons to perpetuate sin was too great a breach and God was public in His response to the gross offense. He told Eli, "All the descendants of your house shall die in the flower of their age. Now this shall be a sign to you that will come upon your two sons, on Hophni and Phinehas: in one day they shall die, both of them. Then I will raise up for Myself a faithful priest who shall do according to what is in My heart and in My mind. I will build him a sure house, and he shall walk before My anointed forever" (1 Samuel 2:33-35). Their vile acts aborted destiny and also short circuited their father's. The entire family was affected.

Priests served as advocates who went before God for the people. When they became contaminated, the nation was in a perilous state. If a high priest was derelict in his duties, someone had to set things in order. God will not allow anyone called to this office to defile themselves and continue serving. He cares too much about the well being of His people. When Eli erred, God stepped in and removed him. King Hezekiah determined not to suffer the same fate.

During his reign, it became his mission to ensure the Temple was purified and worship reinstated. He knew the sins of his people brought judgment and suffering, and did what he could to reverse the curse. In the first month, Hezekiah opened the doors of the temple, repaired them, brought in the priests and Levites, and assembled them. They were required to remove all defilement from themselves and the temple.

The Levites consecrated the utensils, and offered a sin offering for the Kingdom, the sanctuary, and Judah. They knelt and worshipped with music and singing. Hezekiah wanted to safeguard the spiritual health of the nation (2 Chronicles 29). He made a new covenant with God.

It was the ruler's duty to establish order. They issued decrees to ensure priests were properly positioned to draw and maintain blessings over the kingdom. Sometimes it was the other way around. Jehoiada, the priest, protected the kingdom. He hid King Joash, son of Ahaziah, in the temple for six years, and made sure he was crowned King (2 Chronicles 28, 29).

Kings had major influence if priests were lax in their
responsibility.

An anointed priest protects the king. Jehoiada resolved that
God's choice for king would be crowned, and they would govern
(2 Chronicles 23:3). He then gave the Levites specific
instructions to ensure no harm came to the king (2 Chronicles
23:7). Jehoiada also appointed the Levitical priests back to
their rightful place to protect the sanctity of the temple. These
actions established peace in the land. Protecting the kingly
anointing benefited the entire Kingdom (2 Chronicles 29:16-
21).

The permanent priest. Jesus Christ "became a priest not on the
basis of a regulation as to his ancestry but on the basis of the
power of an indestructible life" (Hebrews 7:16). He was
described as,

> One who is holy, blameless, pure, set apart from sinners,
> exalted above the heavens. Unlike the other high priests,
> he did not need to offer sacrifices day after day, first for his
> own sins, and then for the sins of the people. He sacrificed
> his life for the sins of mankind once and for all when he
> died on the cross. For the law appoints as high priests men
> in all their weakness; but the oath, which came after the
> law, appointed the Son, who has been made perfect forever
> (Hebrews 7:26-28).

You have access to uncommon favor and divine protection
through that indestructible life.
    Jesus is your everlasting Prophet, King and Priest. He will
tell you of things to come. The God of all peace is your Savior.
It is because of Him that you have power to draw the oil.
Accepting His sacrifice positions you to be chosen and anointed.
He continually prays for you. The anointing oil is sacred and
there are specific requirements you must meet to qualify.

THE OIL

The oil carries unfiltered, undiluted and uncontaminated power therefore the process of qualification is arduous. The power cannot be transferred from one individual to another. You must become equipped by persevering through God-designed hardships or overcoming demonically orchestrated persecutions. The anointing is not bestowed casually. It is imparted to those who have qualified in their process. The weight of responsibility can be overwhelming.

The anointing does not make you immune from attack. It provides fortification or weaponry to withstand the assault, to launch an offensive or to restore the anointed. Prophets, priests and kings are made in this process. The Word of God gives sustenance to keep the oil flowing as you are being shaped and built to serve.

Consider the essentials of the oil. Olives were shaken, beaten and pressed. Myrrh was scraped from the tree. It contains a cleansing element, agents to ward off infection or kill bacteria, and also boosts the immune system.[2] There are sweetening ingredients (cinnamon and calamus). One of the oils would not be possible without constant saturation at the roots of the plant (Cassia).[1] All five are necessary for the oil to have maximum power. Each component was carefully chosen by God.

Moses was advised about the ingredients to include as well as the precise measurements he should use. Specifically, "500 shekels of liquid myrrh, half as much (that is, 250 shekels) of fragrant cinnamon, 250 shekels of fragrant calamus, 500 shekels of cassia—all according to the sanctuary shekel—and a hin of olive oil" (Exodus 30:22-24). Each part contained something vital to the potency of the oil:

- *Myrrh.* "Myrrh is a necessary ingredient in embalming fluid."[1] After the flesh is dead, it purifies the body and removes the overwhelming stench of death. It has "antiseptic and astringent properties; antiseptics kill bacteria and astringents cleanse. It can be used to treat wounds and also has "immune boosting properties." [2]

155

- *Cinnamon.* "Cinnamon is a spice used to add a sweet smell to the anointing oil; it provides both flavor and fragrance. It also can act as an antibacterial agent and be used to treat infection." [3]

- *Cane.* "Cane, or Calamus, is used to sweeten the anointing oil." [1] "It is also used to increase circulation."[4]

- *Cassia.* The branches of the cassia herb retain moisture and must be planted in a swampy area near the banks of a river in order to survive. [1] This plant's roots needs to be constantly saturated with water. "It kills bacteria and helps to fight disease."[6]

- *Olive Oil.* "The process required to get olive oil is painful and intense. First, the trunk of the olive tree must be shaken harshly, causing the olives to fall to the ground. Then the olives must be beaten and smashed until the liquid runs out. The oil is used both to dress wounds and, in the Jewish tradition, to anoint objects or vessels that are earmarked to be used for the glory of God." [1]

Instructions had to be followed precisely. God knew exactly what would be needed to make, sustain and restore the power of those He anointed.

"Cinnamon, calamus and cassia (in powder form), and myrrh (crushed and mixed with oil). All were added to the olive oil, 12 ½ pounds of myrrh, 6 ¼ pounds of cinnamon, 6 ¼ pounds of calamus, 12 ½ pounds of cassia, and a gallon of olive oil."[5] Anything in powder form was ground from its former state. The creation process required pressure, crushing and stirring.

In my research I learned that the cassia was also a type of cinnamon,[6] so there were equal portions of everything needed for the anointed to - stand, endure, fight, soothe and heal - mixed with the oil. In this, God was extremely considerate. There was an equal amount of fragrance included because He knows what those He anoints will suffer as they live to fulfill destiny.

The fragrance of the anointing is drawn to those who need its power. Herz maintains, "perfumery can be likened to the nose as music is to the ear."[7] The fact that a sweet smelling fragrance is compared to music is significant. Music provides warmth, reassurance and joy, not only to the human ear, but to the mind, spirit and body. It is like a salve, a missing ingredient added at just the right time, in just the right amount. It soothes, comforts, and refreshes. The fragrance of the anointing, coupled with its power, preserved prophets like Jeremiah in the most difficult times.

"Spices used to make the oil were found in the wilderness, a place where separation and trials are encountered;"[8] a place that served as a proving ground. It is where David found himself. He was the shepherd king, still in phases of trials and qualification. "He paid a great price *after* he was anointed. He was sent back to his old position,"[8] on the back side of the hills to tend the animals after what seemed like the end of his validation process. David was taking care of sheep with the weight of the anointing resting upon him. "Everything having to do with his life had to do with the anointing."[8]

Wilderness experiences increase the anointing. Jesus went through the process of preparation on the way to destiny. He was crowned King at birth, yet has proven himself time and time again. He found Himself in the wilderness, completely separated, vulnerable and challenged to stand (Matthew 4:1-11). The same was true of John. He was called from birth, but went through a tough process of preparation (Luke 1:80). It was the ability to sustain a lifestyle of worship in their trial which proved to be the final qualifier.

It is important for bodies to be rested, and spirits rejuvenated so they can be refueled. This gives them strength and fortitude to complete the work. John had the honor of baptizing Jesus and experienced a crowning moment when the Presence of God rested upon Him. Jesus' feet were anointed with oil; these times created respites from the weight of ministry. There are other ways to refresh the spirit, one of which also provides supernatural sustenance. It is the dew of Heaven. Let us look at this briefly.

THE DEW

Heavenly dew revitalizes the spirit. It reinforces individuals bearing the anointing and ensures the potency and longevity of the oil. It purifies and refreshes, provides nourishment, increases the potential for prosperity, gives new life, causes growth and vitality, and drapes a blessing over the anointed as it falls. The atmosphere must be right for dew to form and descend.

Spirits become shriveled and are essentially lifeless as a result of sustained and intense battles. Anyone engaged in persistent warfare or other prolonged physical exertion needs to be restored and refreshed to continue to be effective. In Isaiah 26:19, the [Lord's] dew is referred to as, "A dew of [sparkling] light [heavenly, supernatural dew]" that will restore life to dead bodies" (AMP). When it rests, new sparks of life are created.

Dew sustains provision. In the wilderness, the children of Israel grumbled and complained against Moses and Aaron. Despite their attitude, God provided for them in a time of need. The dew sustained their provision and preserved what God provided as nourishment. It was kept fresh until it could be consumed (Exodus 16:13-14).

Dew also manifested in Isaac's blessing over Jacob. He proclaimed substantial provision in Jacob's life (Genesis 27:28). He called for "heaven's dew" to draw abundance. His desire was for it to not only bring abundance, but also maintain it throughout Jacob's lifetime. He wanted the blessing of God to be present in his son's life. Those blessings were eventually realized.

Dew symbolizes favor. Proverbs 19:12, describes the kings favor as "dew on the grass." The kings favor saved Queen Esther's life (Esther 5). It released Nehemiah to rebuild the walls of Jerusalem (Nehemiah 2), and supplied Daniel with authority, protection and provision throughout three monarchies (Book of Daniel). The king's favor positioned Joseph to provide for his family, and his nation (Genesis 41:39-

44). It was favor that sent a tiny baby here to eventually die so that you could be redeemed from the curse of sin and death. This favor is available to you today as you work to advance the Kingdom of God through the power of His anointing (Isaiah 18:4).

The dew as favor is like a garment that snugly fits at first then stretches over time as you wear it. God said, "I will be like the dew to Israel; he will blossom like a lily. Like a cedar of Lebanon he will send down his roots; his young shoots will grow. His splendor will be like an olive tree, his fragrance like a cedar of Lebanon. People will dwell again in his shade; they will flourish like the grain, they will blossom like the vine— Israel's fame will be like the wine of Lebanon" (Hosea 14:5-7).

He spoke of blessings, security, stability, authority, wealth and prosperity, and a notoriety that would establish Israel as His chosen people. Allow the dew to saturate your life and those things can be spoken of you as well. Drape yourself with the garment and see the anointing increase.

THE GARMENT

It is important to know exactly what God has anointed you to do. Stay in your lane. Do not be easily swayed from your assignment. God provides the garment. He dresses the priest. He speaks to the prophet. He equips the king to rule.

In Zachariah chapter three, the High Priest (Joshua) was dressed by the angel of God in preparation for ministry. His filthy garments identified the unpreparedness to serve. He had to be transformed in order to function in the priestly anointing.

God protects His anointed. Satan stood to accuse Joshua and God stepped in, saying, "The LORD rebuke you, Satan! The LORD, who has chosen Jerusalem, rebuke you! Is not this man a burning stick snatched from the fire?" (Zechariah 3:2). Joshua had been marked for service by God, and the Lord would not allow the enemy access to him at such a critical time of preparation.

God's instructions were clear. He selected Joshua to govern His house but it required obedience (Zechariah 3:7). Not only would Joshua govern, but he would also walk in great dimensions of spiritual authority, serving as one of God's messengers. To qualify for that calling, a process of purification was necessary.

Joshua's entire spiritual identity took on a new form. His dirty garments were replaced with clean ones. He was adorned in the glory and suffering of his anointing. Joshua's mind had to be prepared; the removal of sin was not enough to sustain the anointing. His thinking had to change.

It is impossible to hear the heart of God when your mind is clouded by old thought patterns and strategies. They have the potential to delay or abort destiny and derail God's purposes. You feel compelled to try to have it your way. God could not elevate him unless his mind was transformed (Zechariah 3:5). He would now become a pure conduit for revelation.

A lifestyle of worship and a spirit of prayer safeguard the anointing. The power of the priestly anointing manifests through obedience, humility, transformation, suffering, submission to the perfect will of God and a keen sense of responsibility to live a life worthy of the call. This is not possible unless you continually study and meditate on the Word of God. Spend time on the threshing floor, the place of winnowing and separation which leads to consecration and total surrender. This will increase not only the level of oil in your life, but also the magnitude and importance of each assignment given. "Grow in the grace and knowledge of our Lord and Savior Jesus Christ" (2 Peter 3:18) so that you are able to combat the enemy from a position of full spiritual authority. No demonic activity can prevail.

Jesus walked in this dimension of spiritual authority. He performed miracles consistently. He was not moved by interfering spirits. His work was blessed, and the people whose lives He transformed were blessed. Individuals connected to them were blessed. Do not allow yourself to become contaminated. Be positioned at all times to carry the mantle for the cause of Christ. Become a vessel, prepared to receive the blessing.

THE BLESSING

"If you fully obey the LORD your God and carefully follow all his commands I give you today, the Lord your God will set you high above all the nations on earth. All these blessings will come on you and accompany you if you obey the LORD your God" (Deuteronomy 28:1-2). This proclamation was spoken to the children of Israel. What followed were very specific pronouncements of blessings on the fruit of their womb, their crops, and livestock.

They would be undefeated in battle and enjoy unequalled prominence among nations (Deuteronomy 28:3-14). The promised measure of prosperity which came as a result of obedience was beyond compare. Consequences of disobedience were also clear (Deuteronomy 28:15-65). You can experience a wealth of blessings if you obey God's commands.

Obedience provides full access to your blessings. Someone who is anointed, yet chooses to disobey will face grave repercussions, much like Jonah did. He was swallowed by a giant fish (Jonah 1) until his spirit began governing again. Adam and Eve disobeyed too, and lost their home. Rather than a blessing, they received a lifetime of hardship (Genesis 3). God's grace was present in both situations, but the anointing was not at work. It had been obscured by man's self will. It is better to obey (1 Samuel 15:22); it is not only the wise thing, it is also the profitable thing.

"The blessing of the Lord, it maketh rich, and He addeth no sorrow to it" (Proverbs 10:22, KJV). Material gain may come as a result of the blessing, but it is the richness of spirit that repels sorrow. If the spirit is not ruling, flesh will govern and produce results that dilute the anointing until it becomes ineffective. "Walk by the Spirit, and you will not gratify the desires of the flesh. For the flesh desires what is contrary to the Spirit, and the Spirit what is contrary to the flesh. They are in conflict with each other, so that you are not to do whatever you want" (Galatians 5:16-17). It is not you, but Christ working in you that provides the certainty of effectual manifestation of His power. It materializes through the anointing and the blessed assurance of activated kingdom authority in the earth. "If we live in the Spirit, let us also walk in the Spirit. Let us not be desirous of vain glory" (Galatians 5:25-26, KJV).

Watch out for pride. It will deflect your blessings onto others who choose to crucify flesh daily. Those are the vessels who are prepared and will not fall away when they are rewarded (Galatians 6:8). Stay in the Spirit. Receive directly from the Throne of God. Just as He validated Jesus before men, you too will hear, "this is my beloved son in whom I am well pleased" (Matthew 3:17).

☩

Prayer

Dear Father, God of Heaven and earth, Creator and Savior, I bow in Your Presence. I humble myself before you; the author and finisher of my faith. I do not wish to be found wanting. Help me to severely crucify the flesh daily. I long to remain pure and holy.

My heart's desire is to serve You and to serve your people. I lay flesh on the altar so that I may enter into the Holy of Holies, unencumbered. My life is Yours, my heart and soul, my will – are Yours. Use me as You wish. I submit myself for both the bitterness and the sweetness of my process. Pour the oil. Pour the oil, Lord. I drape myself in the garments of prayer, praise and worship. I stand ready to receive the blessing.

This I cannot do without you, Lord. Remain with me always. In Jesus' name, Amen.

Chapter Eight
❧
THE BLESSING OF THE DOVE

The blessing of the Dove will rest on those who have willingly gone through the process of purification; the ones who are humble and wholly surrendered to God. They walk in humility, obedience and submission. They live a lifestyle of worship and devotion, having endured the suffering in their process. They are equipped to handle the benefits, responsibilities and rewards of the anointing.

David understood the value of his affliction. He realized it served to work all of the required principles into his spirit. He knew it continually prepared him for assignments, battles and tests. He expressed this, saying, "Let a righteous man strike me—that is a kindness; let him rebuke me—that is oil on my head" (Psalm 141:5).

David discerned the significance of his process. Shemei the Benjamite publicly cursed and stoned him while he was running from persecution (2 Samuel 16:10-13), and he yielded to his cross. He put his arms out, head back, body straight, feet slightly apart and planted against the wood, and said, "Nail me to my cross. I may flinch, I may cry out; I know the pain will be excruciating, but nail me to my cross. There are blessings on the other side for me. I will suffer for something greater—nail me to my cross." Imagine yourself being at that point. What would you do?

I picked up a book a few months ago because I was intrigued by the title. It read "No Cross, No Crown." That spoke volumes to me. I have often heard the saying, "No guts, no glory" and understood it to mean there is a price one must pay to become great. You have to go through trials to develop stature and maintain status as a great servant of God. You have to endure to walk in spiritual authority and carry an anointing to transform atmospheres.

Jesus was the ultimate example, a premium sacrifice. The patriarchs of the Bible came through their cross bearing experience, because of the anointing. It holds a power which creates willingness, desire, and conviction to suffer for a cause. Apostle Trevor Banks once made a distinction between having a preference to do something and having a conviction to do it. Preference is a desire for it, but conviction drives you to move; to transform your circumstances. When there is a conviction to do something, you act resolutely, no hesitation.[1]

Be resolved to do whatever it takes to be positioned for the Blessing of the Dove (Holy Spirit). The reward will be greater than the process. It is much like a woman giving birth. The pain seems unbearable in the moment, but the joy of that little baby surpasses all hurt and leaves something beautiful in its place. You are never alone in your process; God has equipped you with everything you need. Hang in there, your end will be greater than your beginning.

To withstand a prolonged process of persecution, you need power. The Blessing of the Dove provides active and reserve power to endure tests. The level of testing Jesus experienced required an enormous amount of that power. He was blessed by His Father, and it magnified His anointing. He was subjected to a protracted and unrelenting attack in a barren place, for over forty days with no food, but active power resisted the attack.

At the end of the test, the enemy got close as he attempted to contaminate what he saw as a vulnerable spirit. He did not understand that Jesus carried a spiritual reservoir containing a substantial amount of reserve power. If you plug into God and allow Him to make you, your spiritual reservoir will also be full.

The blessing of the Dove anoints the commissioned and shuts

down opposition to purpose. Jesus was well equipped to face his adversary and withstand him. Forty days of fasting created a spiritual environment where the devil could only try, but would never succeed. At the end of the wilderness experience, there was a progression of exhibited power in Jesus' words. They came straight from the Word of God. Satan could not contend with that power (Matthew 4:1-11). Speak the Word with spiritual authority; you will have the same results.

David endured his process. Because his attitude remained right in the midst of it all, he was eventually restored to his throne. Jesus endured His process and after three days rose again, with greater power. Today He sits at the right hand of God. Do not run from the scourging that will surely come. Participate in the process by submitting yourself to God. Your anointing will be greater, accurately positioning you for the blessing.

Jacob placed himself where he could take Esau's blessing. He received it, using deception and suffered for a long time afterwards (Genesis 27). Do not take this path. Be rightly positioned to avoid delay to the fulfillment of purpose. Don't forfeit what God has determined is your portion.

"There are two things that must come to an end for you to be positioned properly: First, the devil must stop getting victory on the inside of you (pride, rebellion, or strife) and second, sin must come to an end."[2] If sin continues to have dominion over you, the devil is able to defeat you until you are no longer accurately positioned to receive the blessing of the Dove. Preparation begins with the purification process.

Positioned for the Blessing
Purification. To qualify for the blessing of the Dove the spirit must be pure. If the spirit is pure and governing, the soul and life will be pure. This produces a walk that draws the blessing of the Dove. Malachi 3:1-3 says,

> I will send my messenger, who will prepare the way before me. Then suddenly the Lord you are seeking will come to his temple; the messenger of the covenant, whom you desire, will come," says the LORD Almighty...He will be like

a refiner's fire or a launderer's soap. He will sit as a refiner and purifier of silver; he will purify the Levites and refine them like gold and silver. Then the LORD will have men who will bring offerings in righteousness.

Purification brings the blessing and the anointing of the oil in abundance. God validates you as a Kingdom ambassador, bestowing grace, authority and the power to impact those to whom you have been assigned. Purification comes through repentance (Matthew 3:2, Acts 3:19), humility (Psalm 25:9, Psalm 149:4), obedience (1 Peter 1:22) and surrender (Romans 12:1). One cannot be an effective vessel without these principles.

Humility. Jesus had no pride in His heart. He was not compelled to seek status or glory in man's adulation. When people prematurely sought to elevate Him, He hid Himself from them. Jesus did not seek approval or notoriety. He performed miracles, saying, "tell no one" (Mark 7:36). He was the epitome of humility.

He faced His accusers, yet bore no offense. He fully obeyed His Father and had faith to believe all things were possible. Because He qualified for the anointing and the assignment, He was properly positioned to receive grace.

Obedience. Knowing that he was validated by God freed Jesus to live as The Father willed. He spoke truth without fear of repercussions. He handled rejection and abandonment yet did not develop issues with self image. He only displayed anger when His Father's Temple was defiled. There was no guile or bitterness in Him. He was betrayed, yet served with love. He was beaten and hung on a cross, yet offered forgiveness. He was reviled by men, but reviled not.

To receive the blessing of the Dove, you must follow the path of Christ. Develop a relationship with God as He did. Live as He lived. Obey, even when you are called to do difficult things. What Jesus was asked to do (offer His life) was hard, but He was obedient in spite of the cost. Submit to the will of God completely, no matter what that means. It prepares you for the blessing of the Dove.

Submission. Immediately after Jesus was baptized and validated (Mark 1:11-12), the blessing strengthened His resolve to do His Father's will. He had power to withstand temptation. Some say, "Of course He did; He was the Son of God." It is important to remember He came to earth as a man, with fleshly vices which he had to overcome daily. He had a strong prayer life, because He needed to be close to God, to speak to Him often and maintain staying power. It was His ultimate act of worship.

Worship and Devotion. Jesus Christ was without sin, yet He saturated Himself with the Word. It was so ingrained in His spirit that the power of the anointing magnified and produced miracle after miracle. God's blessing caused Him to stand and proclaim without fear of rejection. He and the Father were one, therefore He was never alone.

You have access to the same assurance. When the enemy confronts you, pull out the stored weaponry (the Word on the inside of you) and send him back to hell. At the end of it all, your body may feel weary but your spirit man will be rejuvenated, and angels will minister to you as your spiritual reserves refuel (Matthew 4:11).

The Word and the power were in Christ because of worship and devotion. Despite His suffering, there was peace and grace; a grace which brought favor and strength to move into full Kingdom authority.

You have power, strength, grace and victory if you carry the anointing. These are all ingredients in the life of an individual on whom the oil has been poured. Nothing can prevent you from establishing the Kingdom in the earth realm. You become a conduit for the out workings of the anointed power of God.

GRACE

Grace is a gift. "When you get into oppressive dimensions, you must know how to fight. Grace enables you. It will make the weak become strong, cause confusion to cease, touch your body, and keep you young and vibrant."[3] Jesus died that you might live; He suffered that you may endure. Grace held His body on the cross and gave Him strength through the beatings, piercings, spitting, and ripping flesh.

Grace was at work as He suffered. Grace was in the Garden of Gethsemane where He prayed alone, asking for strength to carry the burden of the sacrifice all the way to the end. Grace reached out and changed the heart of a thief in his final hours (Luke 23:32-43). It reached down to a soldier at the foot of the cross and transformed his life forever (Matthew 27:54). You are an heir to that grace (Hebrews 4:16).

Grace births and enhances the ability to walk uprightly. Stephen was "A man full of God's grace and power, [who] performed great wonders and signs among the people. Opposition arose…but they could not stand up against the wisdom the Spirit gave him as he spoke" (Acts 6:8-10). Those who opposed him concocted lies to discredit him, though he was innocent. They wanted cause to harm him (Acts 6:11). Even then, grace was present. It was anchored so securely in Stephen's spirit, nothing could dislodge it. Their accusations carried a penalty of death; yet he was not shaken (Acts 6:15). There was no fear in his heart because he knew grace.

Grace was like a grounding rod of steel in Stephen's spirit. The Sanhedrin wanted him dead because he spoke freely about God. They could not terrify him into saying what they wanted. When it became clear they would kill him, grace exuded love and forgiveness toward his false accusers. It became a radiant shroud in the last seconds of his life (Acts 7:55-60).

As they stoned Stephen, grace touched "a young man named Saul" (Acts 7:58) in whose heart it would begin to work. He would become one of the greatest Apostles of that time. Saul was changed forever, and in the transformation, he received a new name. He would be called Paul. He went on to win many souls for the Kingdom.

As Paul's relationship with the Lord grew, God told him, "My grace is sufficient for thee: for my strength is made perfect in weakness" (2 Corinthians 12:9). When that revelation was shared, it was because he had been asking God to remove his suffering. Grace developed a shift in his spirit and eventually he received power to endure (2 Corinthians 12:9-10). Power manifested because of grace. It is available to everyone (Ephesians 4:7). Be careful not to deflect it with a prideful spirit.

Grace protects the anointing of the humble and obedient. When your heart becomes burdened as a result of the suffering endured in your process, grace helps you to stand and persevere until you are on the other side of the experience. It walks you through the fire and holds your head up above the flood. The Bible says, "God resisteth the proud, but giveth grace unto the humble" (James 4:6). If you wear the garment of humility, and, "Submit yourself to God, [when you] resist the devil; he will flee from you" (James 4:7). Satan has no choice, because grace brings exponential power. It is a power which defeats the fiercest foe and draws favor into the lives of those on whom it rests.

FAVOR

God insulates His anointed. You will face challenges and battles, or have victories and great triumphs. God's favor is a shield of protection at all times as you move in power. King David spoke intimately of this favor because He had been a recipient of it throughout his lifetime. He said, "Surely, LORD, you bless the righteous; you surround them with your favor as with a shield" (Psalm 5:12). He testified to many encounters where God's hand protected him.

Obedience and humility cause you to grow in favor. At age twelve, when Jesus' parents found Him in the Temple Courts sitting among the teachers, they expressed concern. He could have rebelled. Instead, "He went down to Nazareth with them and was obedient to them...And Jesus grew in wisdom and stature, and in favor with God and man" (Luke 2:51-52). Humility and obedience brought Him favor. His actions were observed and appreciated. Favor gradually developed in the hearts of the people.

169

Love and faithfulness gain favor. Expressing love to your fellow man, and displaying faithfulness to the work of the Lord, will cause you to gain favor. King Solomon said this, "Let love and faithfulness never leave you; bind them around your neck, write them on the tablet of your heart. Then you will win favor and a good name in the sight of God and man" (Proverbs 3:1-4). If you consistently incorporate these principles into your life, and adopt behavior done out of a heart of service, favor will always be available to you.

Favor manifests at divinely appointed times. God gave a promise to Abraham and Sarah. He said He would give them a son. This promise was made long after they were past child bearing years. To assure them it would come to pass, He said, "I will return to you at the appointed time next year, and Sarah will have a son" (Genesis 18:14). To Abraham and Sarah, the manifestation seemed highly unlikely. Sarah laughed when she heard the pronouncement. They had trouble believing, but God does not lie (Numbers 23:19). He did what He promised, at the appointed time (Genesis 21:1-2).

The period from promise to manifestation ultimately brings some suffering. It was difficult for Abraham and Sarah to wait. They often vacillated between unbelief and hope as each day passed. If they shared the promise with anyone who had the smallest doubt, they probably dealt with the agonizing, often asked question, "Has anything happened yet?" It was hard, but the end of those agonizing days brought them closer and closer to the promise.

SUFFERING

If you are anointed, you will suffer for the cause of Christ, and why not you? (Philippians 1:29). Warriors have an expectation of harm or death during battle; you are not exempt. There is a misconception that the Blessing of the Dove will ensure no hardships are endured. The Apostle Paul testifies to the invalidity of this presumption, stating that he had, "Been in prison...been flogged...and exposed to death again and again" (2 Corinthians 11:23). Your hardships may not be as severe, but they will exist nonetheless. Do not be fearful or run from purpose because you wish to avoid the inevitable.

Paul was anointed to suffer. During his conversion, he was brought to the house of the disciple Ananias. He had a vision that Paul had specifically been chosen, not just to advance the Kingdom of God, but also to suffer for Him (Philippians 1:12-14). Knowledge of the anointing to suffer encouraged and strengthened others who also fearlessly began speaking of the gospel of the Kingdom. Along with Christ, Paul was also an example of how to suffer for the Kingdom (Colossians 1:22). He had firsthand understanding of the pain of affliction, because at one time he was the one tormenting God's anointed servants.

You will suffer for Christ's name, and you can handle it. After his conversion, Paul persevered in anticipation of greater revelations. It was his passion, his focus, his purpose, and it became his strength. He witnessed the repeated resolve of those he once tortured. They remained true to God even though it meant they could lose their lives. At one time Paul thought them foolish, but now he understood. After every beating or imprisonment, his drive to push the gospel across the nations increased. His spirit was as invincible and as unstoppable as those he had persecuted.

Suffering is not uncommon to those who have been called, chosen and anointed. It is a natural part of the process. The pain strengthens the resolve and endurance of the anointed. It may come in the form of persecution from others, or as an affliction (much like Paul's) which serves to compel a perpetual plugging into God. This increases the potency of the anointing and magnifies God's glory to man. Suffering strengthens the spirit of those who are anointed.

STRENGTH AND POWER

The enemy has no power over you, unless you give it to him. You can do all things because of the strength you have through Christ (Philippians 4:13). There is strength for the weary and it increases the power of the weak (Isaiah 40:29). "God stands outside the [world] system, is above the system, and is the law

171

giver of the system. Get your eyes off of other people; they do not have the power."[3] It is God who is all powerful. There is none other. God is the strength of His people, a fortress of salvation for His anointed one (Psalm 28:8). He will make your feet like the feet of a deer and cause you to soar, to excel, and reach heights that you have never imagined (Habakkuk 3:19).

There is power in the name of Jesus, and in His blood. You activate that power every time you say, "Jesus." It is available because of His sacrifice; it works as a result of the anointing. The power is in you; by it you move and have your being. Do not harness it. Operate in a fullness that knows no limitations (Ephesians 2:22). The objective is to allow it to explode into every sphere and realm.

Paul's prayer for the Saints of Ephesus is immensely powerful and it is my prayer for you:

I pray that out of his glorious riches he may strengthen you with power through his Spirit in your inner being, so that Christ may dwell in your hearts through faith. And I pray that you, being rooted and established in love, may have power, together with all the Lord's holy people, to grasp how wide and long and high and deep is the love of Christ, and to know this love that surpasses knowledge— that you may be filled to the measure of all the fullness of God (Ephesians 3:16-19).

"The devil sends persecution or affliction to try the Word that is in you,"[3] but you have been given the power to fight. You have power to subdue, to conquer, to cause the miraculous to manifest, thereby building the Kingdom of God. The Kingdom of Heaven is at hand and it is being expressed through love and supernatural power. His glory will be seen in the life of His anointed ones.

"God is before all things, and by him all things hold together" (Colossians 1:17). He is the "Only wise God full of Glory and majesty, dominion and power both now and ever" (Jude 1:25, KJV). His is the Kingdom and you are a gatekeeper, an ambassador, a warrior, a gatherer. You are called to make that Kingdom known in this earth. You are called to spread the gospel throughout the nations of the world. God has fully equipped you for the Kingdom.

KINGDOM

As a Kingdom ambassador, you have authority to take dominion in the realm of the spirit. Having Kingdom authority does not mean controlling people. The controlling spirit is a spirit of Jezebel that seeks dominance by means of wicked, evil ways. This includes control by manipulation.

Those in true spiritual authority have neither the desire nor the need to control anyone, either directly or subversively. This is never the way of the Kingdom, rather, it is a principle of Lucifer. He exploited Eve in the garden and used the power of suggestion to plant doubt and illicit a desired response. He had no power himself.

Jesus is King, supreme being and ruler of the Kingdom. Power was demonstrated throughout His lifetime. It ushered Him into the end phase of His earthly life where He forged a path to salvation and redemption. His coming heralded the beginning of a new era. Nothing could stop Him. Nothing could prevent the fulfillment of God's plan for mankind.

The Kingdom of God is not weak. Righteously aggressive action will destroy the kingdom of darkness. It not only withstands the enemy, it also overcomes and overtakes him. It is the same authority you carry. You have power to forcefully evict the enemy from your life. Drive him out of territories he has unlawfully taken. They rightfully belong in the Kingdom (Matthew 11:12). Everything he stole will be restored, and everything he attempts to introduce into the King's domain will be demolished.

Satan entered this earthly realm and took vitality, self assurance, courage, strength and peace. He brought pride and introduced doubt, fear, self-will and the desire for self exaltation. He implanted deceitfulness, anger, a spirit of envy, murder and lusts of the flesh. These things repel the anointing, and Satan introduced them because he fears the anointing. It wreaks havoc on the works of darkness and annihilates the plots and plans he devises against the people of God.

Christ's life and power ignited a new generation of Messengers who turned the world upside down with unbridled devotion to the work of the Kingdom. The Apostles and those working alongside them were a source of anointed, focused and unbroken authority, fully sanctioned by Heaven. They taught anyone who would listen, admonished those who doubted, and encouraged those who believed. The Kingdom dimensions were explosive and regenerative; simply unstoppable.

Believe without doubt, advance without fear. Jesus said, "Anyone who will not receive the kingdom of God like a little child will never enter it" (Mark 10:15). If you approach the path of Kingdom advancement and dominion as a child would, victory is assured. If you cannot, you may falter when it is crucial to stand strong. Children believe what you promise. They are excited and expectant. Your nature must be like theirs: bold, daring, unafraid and eager to experience the victory that God has already assured. Do not become a fatality because you hesitate when you should advance—simply believe.

War for the Kingdom. Territories in Kingdoms are taken through conquest. The holder will not relinquish anything. No General goes into war without a strategic battle plan. If the enemy's domain is going to be overrun, you must invade, subdue, conquer and occupy. It is important to know when to hold your peace and when to wage war. The anointing does not abide in your emotions; it comes from a place of peace, but "sometimes there is war before there is genuine peace, and there is no true power without peace. The peace in you must invade your environments."[3]

Protracted wounds and suffering are a natural and predictable part of war. In Acts fourteen, Paul and Barnabas were stoned and left for dead (right after performing a miracle) because they would not allow themselves to be worshiped by the people. The glory belonged to God. As they spoke this truth, the people turned against them. They knew the danger of going into those territories, but they were about Kingdom business.

Paul said, "Through many tribulations we must enter the kingdom of God" (vs. 22). The potential for suffering was acknowledged, but they also believed the anointing would safeguard them.

Discernment and accuracy are tangible assets for Kingdom building. Know your enemy. His history is outlined in the Bible. While his nature is always evident, he is not restricted to old attack methods. He observes his enemy, gleans an understanding of their strategy and forges ahead with tactics designed to render them helpless. His goal is to leave them no viable option, but to surrender, flee or die. Jesus said, "I am sending you out like sheep among wolves. Therefore be as shrewd as snakes and as innocent as doves" (Matthew 10:16). Keep your spirit in tune with the frequencies of Heaven.

Humility safeguards the Kingdom. Do not create openings for a spirit of pride to creep in. Keep the Kingdom anointing potent at all times. Too many people lose the anointing because of pride. You can be God's anointed, yet have no ability to function in your calling. Remember King Saul? He was God's anointed until the day he died, yet his kingly anointing dissipated because of pride, envy, and jealousy. It caused irrational thinking which led to unwise decisions, wrong actions and eventually his downfall. Satan will use whatever is available to him to weaken and attack you. Guard your heart.

Although technology did not always exist, in this era he uses it to pervert and circumvent Kingdom purposes. Television and the internet are used to dismantle confidence and fuel fear. They distribute facts that, while they do not have the power to change your truth according to God's Word, create or adversely affect a weakened belief system. They are also used to introduce overtly graphic acts of violence and an oversaturation of pornographic material. All are designed to permeate spiritual shields and begin a gradual erosion of Kingdom culture.

God's Kingdom is unstoppable. Handle Kingdom business prudently and expeditiously. Jesus described the Kingdom of

Heaven as "Leaven that a woman took and hid in three measures of flour, till it was all leavened" (Matthew 13:33). "Leaven is a substance that makes dough rise and become light. It is said that it is used to produce fermentation." Fermentation is defined as "a transformation or a chemical breaking down to change a substance from one thing to another." In the Kingdom, elements are broken down and transformed so that something or someone can rise. Never forget what you are doing and for whom.

"A little yeast works through the whole batch of dough" (Galatians 5:9). Knowing how much yeast to add is important. Discern the right words; consider the time, and the audience. You are anointed to enter and transform spheres for the Kingdom.

Paul and Barnabas helped the lame man in Acts 14, but it may have been too much "yeast" for that group of people. Instead of seeing God's power, they saw Paul and Barnabas as gods and began to worship them. God has anointed you, and He will tell you what is needed, and when. Listen to Him; act and speak only as He leads. Be careful that your choices are uniting instead of scattering people. There will be instances where this cannot be helped, but complete obedience safeguards you.

The anointing is not self serving. If pride is ruling, the principles which govern are not Christ-like. You deplete rather than increase the Kingdom. Jesus addressed this in Matthew twenty-three when He spoke against the Pharisees who gloried in notoriety and were often found puffing themselves up. They wanted to be seen and to receive pats on the back for their good deeds. He called them hypocrites (Matthew 23:13-15). Those were strong, but necessary, words.

Display the ways of the Kingdom so others can become a part of it. Carry it everywhere you go (Luke 17:21). It's not about you. Through the power of the Holy Spirit, you have the ability to hold on to the anointing. Maintain a pure and humble heart. You can make a great impact for the Lord.

Some people will not celebrate you. There are individuals who will join themselves to you because of the anointing, yet secretly despise you. Others are joyful because of its manifested works, but want nothing to do with you after they have received its touch. Do not be overly sensitive about this. Christ dealt with many of the same attitudes (1 Peter 3:13-16). The behavior is not personal. It is driven by human nature (flesh).

Kingdom purpose will not be stopped. Jesus spoke two parables which expressed the expansiveness of the Kingdom. Saying, "This is what the kingdom of God is like. A man scatters seed on the ground. Night and day, whether he sleeps or gets up, the seed sprouts and grows, though he does not know how. All by itself the soil produces grain—first the stalk, then the head, then the full kernel in the head. As soon as the grain is ripe, he puts the sickle to it, because the harvest has come" (Mark 4:26-29). No demon, no devil, no agents of Satan can stop the advancement of the Kingdom. Do what you are chosen and anointed to do, and leave the rest to God.

The Kingdom will expand at God's will. Jesus further described the Kingdom as "A mustard seed, which is the smallest of all seeds on earth. Yet when planted, it grows and becomes the largest of all garden plants, with such big branches that the birds can perch in its shade" (Mark 4:31-32). You may think the part you play is insignificant, but it is essential. That seed you plant as a result of your obedience to God's will is not yours, it is His. It will multiply until, "The kingdoms of this world are become the kingdoms of our Lord, and of his Christ; and he shall reign for ever and ever" (Revelation 11:15, KJV). You will reign with Him as a joint heir. How marvelous, how wonderful, how magnificent it will be.

The oil has been flowing from the beginning of time, and is still flowing. It was poured out when Adam received God's anointing to have dominion over all the earth. There is a level of saturation that is unparalleled. The oil is flowing today, and the flow provokes intense worship. The entire Kingdom will be bathed in the glory of the King (Philippians 2:10-11). There is music and a heralding of trumpets. There is judgment and war. There is suffering as the enemy unsuccessfully tries again to assume a position he was never anointed to take. In the end,

Kingdom prevails, and the King reigns (Revelation 21:3-5).

Prepare for the oil. Function in its power. Receive validation
from God. You are equipped for the task. You are anointed to
bring the Kingdom of Heaven into the earth. You have been
built for the journey. Jesus is your Everlasting God who was
and is to come (Revelations 1:8). He is the one who anoints and
sustains the anointing. He pours the oil on prepared vessels
ready to live on purpose. When you begin to feel its flow and
see outward manifestations of its power, be assured, you have
risen in stature. Bathe the Heavens with your worship as He
pours the oil on you.

Let it course through veins, through sinews,
Permeating all you are;
Let it render darkness helpless
Advancing nations—near and far
Sacred oil of the anointing
Beacon of the risen Son
At the end of every battle
You will hear Him say, well done
Thea Harris

Prayer
*Oh Most Holy Father, there is none like You. Redeemer of all mankind;
Savior of the world. I am humbled that you found me worthy to be
called, to be chosen. There is nothing I do of myself.*

*Without your anointing, I would fail. Thank you for grace, for favor,
strength and power. Thank you for anointing me to suffer for
Your cause, because without my suffering the potency
of the oil would become compromised.*

*I have learned to trust You in the process. Now Lord, help me please as I
trust You for the labor that is ahead. Continue to equip me for Your
service, and I will forever praise.
In Jesus' name I pray, Amen.*

FINAL WORDS

Every Saint needs the anointing to fulfill purpose. The devil is aware of this and his strategy is thoughtful and devious. When he knew you were called by God, his quest to destroy your identity began. He attacks your mind to destroy purpose, knowing that an individual with no purpose has no power. He attacks your body to impede movement. He may attack your family or your business to distract you. Guard your heart, stay in the Word and saturate yourself in the presence of God.

Identify the contaminants in your life. Search out the hidden things that have become a hindrance. Ask the Lord to reveal them to you, and begin the work of removing them by equipping yourself with tools that have been made available. Be properly positioned to receive the anointing, so it can be protected at all costs.

Know your purpose and stay in your metron to avoid any possibility of renewed contamination. Become consecrated for service. Receive the impartation of the Holy Spirit and accept responsibility of your call. "The LORD bless you and keep you; the LORD make his face shine on you and be gracious to you; the LORD turn his face toward you and give you peace" (Numbers 6:24-26).

If you draw near to God, He will draw near to you (James 4:8). He is a friend who sticks closer than a brother (Proverbs 18:24). Receive the blessing of the Dove. With this blessing comes a suffering designed not to destroy you, but to prepare, equip and anchor you for what is to come. Do not be afraid; He is with you always (Matthew 28:20). Stand in the Holy Place.

Search out His Word for insight and new revelations to fulfill your purpose as an ambassador of the Kingdom. Share the gospel of the Kingdom with the world (Matthew 24:14).

Stand as a true Son/Daughter and Heir as the Kingdoms of this world become the Kingdoms of our Lord and of His Christ. Worship the King; bow in His presence. Receive the anointing of the oil as it is poured out upon you. Go tell the world about Jesus, your Savior, Redeemer and King. As you move in purpose, "May the grace of the Lord Jesus Christ, and the love of God, and the fellowship of the Holy Spirit be with you" (2 Corinthians 13:14). God will be pleased, and you will hear Him say, "This is my beloved Son in whom I am well pleased" (Matthew 3:17).

NOTES

Chapter 1: Prepare for the Oil

1. "Questions People Ask About Cancer." American Cancer Society. Full text can be viewed at: http://www.cancer.org/cancer/cancerbasics/questions-people-ask-about-cancer (Accessed on February 15, 2014).
2. "Sound Travels Faster In Water Than In Air." National Oceanic and Atmospheric Administration (NOAA). Full text can be viewed at: http://oceanservice.noaa.gov/facts/sound.html (Accessed on April 28, 2013).
3. Anaya Mandal. "What Is Bone Marrow?" News Medical. Full text can be viewed at: http://www.news-medical.net/health/What-is-Bone-Marrow.aspx (Accessed on April 28, 2013).
4. Mitchell, H.H. "The Water in You." US Geological Survey: The USGS Water Science School. Full text can be viewed at: http://water.usgs.gov/edu/propertyyou.html (Accessed on April 28, 2013).

Chapter 2: Anointing Fall On Me

1. Deborah Gardner, "How to Perform Surgical Hand Scrubs," Full text can be viewed at: http://www.infectioncontroltoday.com/articles/2001/05/how-to-perform-surgical-hand-scrubs.aspx (Accessed on July 1, 2013).

Chapter 3: The Power of the Oil

1. Reinhard Bonnke, "Start Walking in Miracle Working Power," Charisma Magazine. November 15, 2012. Full text can be viewed at: http://www.charismamag.com/spirit/supernatural/15085-the-point-of-your-anointing (Accessed on September 22, 2013).

Chapter 5: The Kingly Anointing

1. Krucik, G. 2013. "Healthline Body Maps: Indept: Abdomen." Full text can be viewed at: http://www.healthline.com/human-body-maps/abdomen (Accessed on January 5, 2014).
2. Wilson, J.L., 2001. Adrenal Fatigue: the 21st century stress syndrome. Petaluma, CA. Smart Publications. pg 290
3. Wilson, J.L., 2001. Adrenal Fatigue: the 21st century stress syndrome. Petaluma, CA. Smart Publications. pg 291
4. Rae, J. n.d. Spiritual Warfare – The Armor of God and Breastplate of Righteousness. Full text can be viewed at: http://www.sharefaith.com/guide/christian-principles/spiritual-warfare/breastplate-of-righteousness.html (Accessed on January 5, 2014).
5. Krucik, G. 2013. Healthline Body Maps: Indept: Vessels. Full text can be viewed at: http://www.healthline.com/human-body-maps/chest#4/1 (Accessed January 6, 2014).
6. Wilson, J. and Christensen, J. 2014. Why Brain Dead Means Really Dead. CNN.com Full text can be viewed at: http://www.cnn.com/2014/01/06/health/brain-dead-basics/ (Accessed on **January 7, 2014**).
7. Schaeffer, D. n.d. What Does Glory Mean. Heart Language. Full text can be viewed at: http://www.intouch.org/magazine/content.aspx?topic=Heart_Language_Glory#.UtGhRfRDvqE (Accessed on January 11, 2014).

Chapter 7: The Priestly Anointing

1. Bynum, J. The Ingredients of the Anointing. Full text can be viewed at: http://www.charismamag.com/site-archives/1367-slw-spiritual-growth-/the-holy-spirit/9399-the-ingredients-of-the-anointing (Accessed on January 20, 2014).
2. Planinz, T.A., 2011. The Benefits of Myrrh Essential Oils. Full text can be viewed at: http://www.livestrong.com/article/395056-health-benefits-of-myrrh-essential-oils/ (Accessed on January 21, 2014).
3. DeVries, L., 2013. Benefits of Cinnamon Oil. Full text can be viewed at: http://www.livestrong.com/article/255284-benefits-of-cinnamon-oil/ (Accessed on January 21, 2014).
4. Ruach, B. 2013. Herbs to Increase Blood Circulation in The Scalp. Full text can be viewed at: http://www.livestrong.com/article/228374-herbs-to-increase-blood-circulation-in-the-scalp/ (Accessed on January 21, 2014).
5. The Holy Anointing Oil. Bible Gateway. Full text can be viewed at:

https://www.biblegateway.com/passage/?search=Exodus+30%3A2 2-33&version=MSG (Accessed on January 21, 2014).

6. Arnold, K. 2013. The Health Benefits of Ceylon vs Cassia Cinnamon. Full text can be viewed at: http://www.livestrong.com/article/516598-the-health-benefits-between-ceylon-cinnamon-and-cassia/ (Accessed on January 21, 2014).

7. Herz, R.S. n.d. Neurobiology of Sensation and Reward: Chapter 17: Perfume. Full text can be viewed at: http://www.ncbi.nlm.nih.gov/books/NBK92802/ (Accessed on January 22, 2014).

8. Banks, T. 2013. Interview: David's Anointing. Fort Pierce, FL. October 1, 2013.

Chapter 8: The Blessing of the Dove

1. Banks, T. 2014. The Faith Crisis Part 6: The Paradox of Faith. Fort Pierce, FL. January 22, 2014.

2. Banks, T. 2013. The Kingdom: Accelerated Progress. Fort Pierce, FL. December 18, 2013.

3. Banks, T. 2014. The Faith Crisis: One Size Fits All. Fort Pierce, FL. February 9, 2014.

ABOUT THE AUTHOR

THEA HARRIS is an author and singer/songwriter from the island of Antigua. Her music releases include *Secret Place*, and the singles *Live Right* and *Intimacy (Into-Me-See)*. She has served as a worshiper for more than 20 years, and is currently working on her sophomore CD due to be released in 2014.

Presently, Thea is a Choir Director and Worship Leader at Resurrection Life Family Worship Center in Fort Pierce, Florida.

For more information go to
www.theaharris.com

WHAT'S NEXT?

Coming soon...
Pour The Oil 40 Day Devotional
Pour The Oil Study Guide

Visit www.theaharris.com for more information

Join The Club
Join the Pour The Oil Book Club on Facebook

https://www.facebook.com/groups/pourtheoil/

Made in the USA
Columbia, SC
08 February 2023

11328124R00117